Just What the DOCTOR Ordered

Soulwinning Stories
by Walter L. Wilson

Bob Jones University Press
Greenville, South Carolina 29614

Just What the Doctor Ordered
by Walter L. Wilson
© 1988 Unusual Publications
1700 Wade Hampton Boulevard
Greenville, South Carolina 29614

Printed in the United States of America.
95 94 93 92 91 90 89 88 5 4 3

Library of Congress Cataloging-in-Publication Data

Wilson, Walter L. (Walter Lewis), 1881-1969.
   Just what the doctor ordered.

   1. Wilson, Walter (Walter Lewis), 1881-1969.
2. Evangelists—United States—Biography.
3. Evangelistic work. I. Title.
BV3785.W616A3 1988   269'.2'0924 [B]   87-37167
ISBN 0-89084-439-9

Cover design by Anne R. Peck
Illustration by James A. Brooks

Contents

Publisher's Note

The stories in this volume, with only minor editorial changes, have come from four of Wilson's books: *The Romance of a Doctor's Visits, Miracles in a Doctor's Life, Strange Experiences of the Doctor,* and *Doctor Wilson's Stories of Soulwinning.* The Publisher would like to express appreciation to Mr. Wade Ramsey, a grandson of Walter Wilson, for his help and advice in this project and to Mrs. Walter Wilson for presenting the opportunity to bring some of her husband's stories back into print and thus hold up before a new generation the warm heart and faithful service of this fine soulwinner.

Biographical Sketch of Walter L.Wilson

"Yes, that is my principal business in life." This is how Dr. Walter Wilson would often respond when some troubled soul asked him if he could explain how to get to heaven. His words take on special meaning when one realizes how varied were this man's talents and how wide his experiences—medical doctor, natural scientist, salesman, businessman, author, preacher, school administrator, and more. Yet in every activity his consuming passion was to help needy souls find eternal life.

Walter Lewis Wilson was born in Aurora, Indiana, May 27, 1881. In some ways he followed in the footsteps of his father, a druggist who turned to preaching and doctoring. Tragedy struck early, though, for Walter's mother died shortly after his first birthday, and he went to live with his grandparents in Fort Smith, Arkansas, for the next nine years. In 1891 the Wilson home was once again united when his father remarried and settled down in Kansas City, a town destined to become Walter's base of operations for most of his long life.

While still very young, Wilson showed a strong interest in religion. He joined a Methodist church in Kansas City, but the church, being liberal, did not preach the gospel. Although he realized his need of God, he had not the slightest suspicion that salvation was through grace alone. In fact, he had the firm conviction that he must pay for his sins, and every Sunday he dutifully deposited hard-earned pennies in the offering plate in atonement for his transgressions that week. Then in July 1896, at the invitation of his neighbor, Caleb Baker, he attended a tent meeting sponsored by the Plymouth Brethren. There the preacher hammered home the truth that no man can attain righteousness before God by his own works. Young Wilson had to admit that the Bible seemed to teach what the man said, yet he struggled with the idea. Six months later he showed up at another tent meeting. On his way home after the service, having sat down on a bench in front of a saloon to mull over the message he had heard, he gave his heart to the Lord Jesus Christ.

Wilson's life was never the same, and he began thinking seriously about the ministry. A preacher from Scotland named Donald Ross befriended the teenager with spiritual advice and encouragement and, on his deathbed, prayed that God would raise him up to succeed him. The next year, still in high school, Wilson began holding street meetings in Kansas City, and he soon demonstrated the creative approach to evangelism that would mark his entire ministry. One day, for instance, he placed a derby hat upside down on the sidewalk and covered it with a white handkerchief. When a crowd had gathered in curiosity around the unusual object, Wilson began to preach. He followed the same method in personal soulwinning, often making some out-of-the-ordinary comment or mentioning an obscure passage of Scripture in an unusual context to excite the listener's curiosity. He would then lead into the presentation of the gospel.

After high school Wilson studied to be a doctor at the University Medical School of Kansas City. Because he was colorblind, he had to take an additional year at Northwestern University Medical College in Chicago before he could obtain his license to practice. Lack of financial help from his family made his student years difficult, but by dint of hard work, economizing, and native business sense he made it through.

He married soon after graduation and set up practice in Webb City, Missouri. His bride was Marion Baker, youngest daughter of Caleb Baker, the neighbor who had persuaded

Wilson to go to the tent meetings where he heard the gospel. The courtship, which lasted eight years, had begun after Marion's older sister Jessie had refused to date Walter any more because he had shown up for a date wearing a tie that clashed horrendously with his suit. Poor colorblind Walter had had no inkling of the reaction his outfit would receive, but he was able to put his grief aside when Marion showed a willingness to replace her sister.

Wilson's relationship with the Baker family had other far-reaching results. Marion's father was involved in the tentmaking business, the Baker-Lockwood Manufacturing Company to be specific. A few months after his daughter's wedding, Baker became bedridden with osteomyelitis. He then requested that Wilson, who had worked with him part-time while in college, come help out at the plant during his illness. Wilson assented reluctantly, but by the time Baker recovered he had become an integral part of the company. So for twenty-five years Wilson helped manage and served as an agent for the Baker-Lockwood Company, and this occupation forms a backdrop for many of the soulwinning experiences he relates in his books. His extensive traveling in this capacity brought him into contact with people of all walks of life, including some famous ones like "Buffalo" Bill Cody and John Ringling of the Ringling Circus.

Although he never received ordination or even formal Bible training, Wilson eventually became well known as a Bible teacher. His connection with the Lord's work came in many ways. In 1920 he was a leader in the formation of Central Bible Hall in Kansas City, a nondenominational church organized somewhat along the lines of Plymouth Brethren assemblies, and eventually he served as its pastor. He also led in the establishment of the Flagstaff Indian Mission, which the church sponsored to bring the gospel to the Navahos in the Southwest. In 1924 he became a pioneer in the field of radio preaching when WOQ of Kansas City began broadcasting a live, half-hour lesson by Wilson every Sunday. The next year it became a daily program at breakfast time six days a week. He also helped in the founding of Kansas

City Bible College, which later became Calvary Bible College, and he served as president and in other capacities when needed through the years. At first Walter Wilson's ministry as a Bible teacher had only a limited scope. Then in the early 1930s Harry Ironside, pastor of the Moody Memorial Church in Chicago, invited him to speak from that platform. Although nervous at the momentous occasion, he was well-received, and, because of the exposure it gave him, invitations to speak began coming from around the country. In the following years he delivered messages at innumerable church services, Bible conferences, summer camps, school assemblies, and civic clubs, to name a few. He was a master at gaining the sympathy and attention of indifferent or even hostile audiences by means of ingenious illustrations. Sometimes humorous, sometimes startling, but always striking, down-to-earth, and to the point, they were his hallmark as a Bible teacher. With his training as a doctor, he found illustrations from the marvels of nature especially appealing. He had an inexhaustible fund of knowledge about the natural world and could on almost any occasion pull out some interesting fact to bring home a Bible truth to the listener.

It was Ironside who suggested to Dr. Wilson in 1935 that he record some of his soulwinning anecdotes for posterity. *The Romance of a Doctor's Visits* was the result, and it was followed by other books along the same line: *Miracles in a Doctor's Life* (1935), *Remarkable New Stories Told by the Doctor* (1940), *Strange Experiences of the Doctor* (1942), and *Doctor Wilson's Stories of Soulwinning* (1959). In addition he wrote a number of Bible study books, children's stories, devotional studies, and soulwinning helps. The most substantial volume was one entitled *Wilson's Dictionary of Bible Types*, an alphabetical listing of various people, objects, and events from the Bible with an explanation of their typological significance.

Marion Wilson died in 1962, having born eight children to the Doctor and faithfully helped him in his remarkable ministry. She was witnessing to a nurse at the moment of her death. The next year, at the age of eighty-two, Wilson married Ruth Selders, graduate of Kansas City Bible College and longtime member of Central Bible Hall. Their time together was short, however, for in the spring of 1969 Wilson suffered a stroke, and he died on May 24.

The stories of Dr. Wilson hold a timeless interest. Although some of the situations are things of the past, his ceaseless concern for the souls of men and women of all ages and stations in life will be relevant as long as there are souls on earth to be won. What is more, he translated that concern into action by taking advantage of every available opportunity to present the gospel. On the other hand, he placed great emphasis on the leading of the Holy Spirit. Each morning he would earnestly pray for the Holy Spirit to guide him to the particular person whom He had prepared to receive the gospel. During the day, expecting God to answer his prayer, he would take advantage of each favorable occasion to speak a word for Christ. He was not one to wait for some strange, inner urging of the Spirit to move him, for the opening up of an opportunity was leading enough for him.

Always a gentleman and never intrusive or abrasive, it was evident that the love of God motivated him. He was not a salesman with a product to huckster onto some unsuspecting potential client. He was not looking for scalps to count. Each one with whom he came in contact was a person who perhaps needed the water of life. He was a man under orders, ready at every moment to follow the Spirit's leading and be the instrument by which God would bring a new-born babe into His kingdom.

—*David Woehr*

Just What the
DOCTOR
Ordered

The Little Man in a Big City

On the fourth day of January, I made a trip to New York City to keep an engagement with a customer. For practical reasons, I decided to register at a hotel near the station and was assigned a room on the eighteenth floor, where the page deposited my baggage. By the time I had refreshed myself and was ready to leave, it was nearly eleven o'clock in the morning. Kneeling beside the bed, I asked the Lord of the harvest to guide me during the day and to use me for His glory. I prayed thus: "My Lord, this is a large city of seven million people, and I am just a weak, unknown servant of Thine with no knowledge of the city and no acquaintance with the hungry hearts that may be here. Thou dost know where the needy ones are. Thou alone dost know whom Thou hast been dealing with. Here is my body—my feet and my lips. Wilt Thou take them today to some troubled heart and speak through me Thy words of light and life? Thank you, Lord. I believe Thou wilt do it."

Rising from my knees, I took my samples, pricebook, and Bible and went out to call on my customer. Walking east on Thirty-second Street, I found near the subway station a stationery shop, in the window of which was a small leather-covered notebook which attracted my attention. I was in need of a new prayerbook, for it was my custom on the first of the year to make out a new list of my petitions to the Lord. The prayer and the date of the petition were placed on the left-hand page, and then a space was kept on the right-hand page in which to write the answer to that prayer and the date on which the reply was received from the Lord. This keeping books with God I found to be most profitable, as well as inspiring and encouraging. Here was the very book that I needed for the new year.

This shop was a very small one and was operated by a German who was very small of stature. As I entered the store, he at once accosted me and desired to know what I would like to purchase. I described the little book in the window and he at once obtained it for me. After a careful examination, I found that it was arranged just right for my needs and agreed to pay the price, $1.10. As he wrapped it up, I asked the Lord whether this might be the person in whose heart He had been working, and I followed the prayer with this inquiry: "Do you know what I expect to do with this little book?"

"No," he said, "unless you vill giff it to some friend for a New Year's present."

"No," I answered, "this will be used as a prayerbook."

A look of surprise and astonishment came over the face of the little German, and he at once began to unwrap the package and to say: "I am sorry, my friend, but you have bought the wrong book. This is a blank book; it is not a prayerbook."

"I know it," I said quickly, feeling that the Lord had given an opening for a conversation about Himself. "You see, I will make my own prayerbook out of this book, for I will write my petitions on the left-hand pages and will enter the answer on the opposite right-hand pages when the Lord gives the answer. I like to keep a record of God's dealings with me and to know whether or not my prayers are being answered."

I observed a deep earnestness and seriousness on the part of my new friend as I told him this story. He finished wrapping the package, placed the money in the cash register, and, still holding the package in his hand, came from behind the counter to talk with me about this matter. Placing the book on the counter and taking hold of the two lapels of my coat, he looked into my face, and I observed tears in his eyes. He was greatly agitated and, with a voice full of emotion, he said, "Can you get to Gott?"

"Yes, indeed," I replied happily. "Many years ago He saved my soul, and since then I have had the joy of knowing Him and walking with Him in happy fellowship. Would you like to find Him?"

It was easy to see that the Holy Spirit had found for me a candidate for glory. How earnestly the little man replied to my question, saying, "Mister, I have tried to find Gott for many years. I have gone around Manhattan and Brooklyn and the Bronx, night after night, attending many services, but failed always to find Gott. Can you tell me how to get to Him?"

"Yes," I replied, "that is my principal business in life. Perhaps you have tried to get to God without going to Him through the Lord Jesus Christ. If you will come to Jesus Christ, He will bring you to God."

I then opened my Bible and read to him John 14:6: "I am the way, the truth, and the life: no man cometh unto the Father, but by me." We also read together 1 Peter 3:18: "Christ also hath once suffered for sins, the just for the unjust, that he might bring us to God."

Here was a heart not far from the kingdom. I remembered the promise of the Lord: "And ye shall seek me, and shall find me, when ye shall search for me with all your heart." Here was one who was seeking, and surely he would find, according to the promise of God. The idea of coming to Christ first as the way to God seemed to be an entirely new thought to my friend. It puzzled him a little, and I saw that it needed an explanation. I sought to show him that there must be a mediator between God and men, and that Christ Jesus was that One. I also sought to show him how the work of Christ at Calvary was quite sufficient to satisfy the demands of God for his sins, and that at Calvary's Cross the Lord Jesus was "wounded for *his* transgressions and

bruised for *his* iniquities" (Isa. 53:5). We read together 1
Peter 2:24: "Who his own self bare our sins in his own body
on the tree." Then we turned to Romans 5:6: "For when
we were yet without strength, in due time Christ died for
the ungodly."

My friend realized that he had no strength, and yet he
was earnestly seeking for the forgiveness of his sins and wanting
access to God as his Father. "How can I find Jesus?" he
asked. "Where can I find Him?"

"You may just accept Him right now, where you are
standing," I assured him. "Just bow your head and tell the
Lord Jesus that you believe in Him, that you love Him, and
that you trust Him just now with your soul's salvation."

He bowed his head at once and said quietly, "Lord Jesus,
I see that You came to die for me and to bring me to God.
I believe in You, and I come to You now with my sins
for You to save me, and I believe that You do. I believe
You will bring me to God, and I trust You with my soul."

My German friend had found the Lord, and the Lord
had found him. The quest of years was at an end. The seeking
heart had found a sufficient Saviour. The one who had been
far off was now made nigh by the blood of Christ. Darkness
had been turned into day, and this friend had passed out
of death into life.

As I left the shop with my prayerbook, I said, "Thank
you, blessed Lord; how quickly You answered my prayer.
How ready You were to take willing feet and a ready heart
and to bring these in touch with the seeking soul. I worship
Thee for this." Looking at my watch, I found that about
twenty minutes had elapsed from the time of the prayer in
the hotel room until the prayer was answered, the work was
finished, and a troubled soul had found peace in Christ.

The Holy Spirit is always ready, waiting, and willing
to lead the yielded servant in paths that are profitable. Let
us learn to look to Him and to depend upon Him, so that
we may be found spending our time wisely and be led by
Him to those hidden hearts in whom He is working.

The Detectives Could Not Find Him

Dr. Leonard was a very prominent pastor in one of our large cities. He was loved by the whole community and honored by the city fathers. He had a son who had come to maturity with a rebellious spirit against the church and, therefore, against his parents. The father and mother sought to help the young man to know the Lord and to love the way of righteousness, but to no avail. He rebelled against "religion," as he called it, and wanted none of it. His parents guarded him very carefully from worldly influences, had him attend church with them regularly, and sought by patience and kindly counsel to bring him to Christ.

The young man endured this for some years, in fact until he had finished his schooling and graduated from college. He then felt that he could safely and properly sever his relationship with his family and go out into the world on his own responsibility. One night he took a few belongings, leaving most of them in his room, and during the night slipped away unseen and unheard. The next morning the parents found his bed had been untouched, and most of his garments were there. His books and many other personal belongings were in their accustomed place, but the traveling bag was gone, and the young man was nowhere to be seen. He dropped out of sight during the night.

The father employed a national detective agency to find the boy. Photographs were sent throughout the country. The homes of his relatives were secretly watched. The mail that went to the relatives was inspected. Telephones were tapped in places where there was a possibility that the boy might be contacted. All of this was to no avail. The lad apparently had just evaporated from society. The father spent a great sum of money seeking to track down his son or to get some information concerning his whereabouts.

It was my privilege to conduct a series of meetings in that city. The church was located near a hospital, and the meetings were attended by patients from the hospital, nurses, and others from different parts of the city. The Spirit of God was moving among the people, hearts were being touched, and each evening there were those who expressed their desire to know the Saviour. On one of these evenings, an usher came to me as I was helping a nurse with a spiritual problem and said, "There is a young man on the front seat who wishes to have a personal visit with you." The nurse had a meeting with the Saviour that evening and returned to the hospital new born and with a new Saviour and a new song. As soon as she left, I went to sit beside the young man, who looked much older than he really was. Here is the story that he related to me:

"Five years ago I slipped away from my home during the night, taking only a few things with me. My father is Dr. Leonard, whom you may have known as the leading preacher of this city. He and my mother were devoted to me and kept insisting that I go with them to the church and participate in the church activities. I rebelled against this program, for I wanted to see the world and to enjoy the things in the world which were denied to me by my parents. I saw other young men who lived as they pleased and seemed to be much happier than I. I felt that, since I was a grown man, I should have the right to live as I pleased, go where I pleased, and do what I pleased. Still, as the preacher's son, I knew it would never be proper for me to go out openly into the ways of the world and thus disgrace my parents.

"After leaving my home, I took up lodging down in the part of a slum district where I thought I could be hidden from the eyes of the godly people who associated themselves with my father's church and with other religious groups. I grew a beard as you see, and this completely disguised my looks. I bought some old clothes at a pawnshop so that I would not be recognized. I went in for sin rather heavily. I began to do all the things I had been wanting to do. I began to drink, to smoke, to carouse generally with others who were living for the devil. I contracted some diseases which are the result of that kind of living. I found it much more difficult to obtain work than I had anticipated and therefore had to live in the cheapest surroundings in filthy rooms and to eat in the cheapest places I could find. Dr. Wilson, I have had five years of that kind of life, all the time knowing and seeing in the papers that my father was making every effort to find me. I knew that my mother was praying, and all the congregation in the church joined in praying that John might be found. I fought my conscience. Bible verses kept coming to my mind reproving me, for I knew very well that I was building up a terrible record which must be met some day at the judgment throne. I made up my mind that I had had all the life of sin that I wanted and was ready to come back to my home and to find the Lord.

"Last night I came to the definite decision to seek some way out of my wicked life and come back to my father and mother. I did not want to return as I was. I wanted to return to them in complete separation from sinful things and with a heart ready to follow the counsel of my father and mother. As I passed along this main street, I noticed the sign in front of this church that a doctor would give an address this evening. I thought that since the address was to be in a church, it would have something to do both with God and with the body. I needed help in both ways, and that is the reason I came to the service tonight. The message you gave was exactly what I needed. So, here I am: tell me what to do."

I read to the young man from Luke 15: "This man receiveth sinners, and eateth with them." I could see that this sweet invitation of our Lord affected his heart. He had been thinking that God would be very severe on him because of his deliberate disobedience to the truths that he had learned. When I saw that this thought was in his heart, I read to him the story of the prodigal son in this same chapter, Luke 15:11-32. I said to him, "You will notice, John, that the father was waiting for his son; he was waiting with kisses, with a ring, with shoes, with a fatted calf, and with a new robe. He was waiting to give a wonderful welcome to his wandering boy. You will notice also, John, that the father said nothing whatever about the path he had taken, the ingratitude, nor the sins that had been committed. The father took the same position as God in the Old Testament when He said to the one who was repentant and returned to God, 'None of his sins that he hath committed will be mentioned unto him' (Ezek. 33:16). The Saviour is waiting for you to come, as you are, just now, and the Saviour will welcome you, and so will the Father Himself."

The tears came to John's eyes. He bowed before the Lord, and, kneeling to Him, he trusted his soul to Christ and gave himself back to his heavenly Father. The work was finished in his soul. As he rose from his knees, he extended both hands to me and said, "I am going straight home now. Probably father and mother have retired, but I will ring the bell, and when the butler comes to the door, I will tell him to tell my parents, 'John has returned home, safe and saved.'" That must have been a wonderful reunion.

The Spirit Worked at Midnight

Our Lord is not limited by time or place in His dealings with lost souls. The Scriptures record divine blessings in the home and on the road, at the pool and in the temple, on a wellcurb and in a treetop; some came by day and some by night. Time is no factor with the Lord when the fate of a soul is at stake.

There lived in a certain city a young Christian woman with an unsaved husband. This husband was not very friendly to Christian things; in fact, he opposed and hindered his wife in her desire to serve the Lord and to attend the meetings of Christians. It was the old story of a divided house. The husband was not always passively opposed but sometimes was quite hostile in his attitude toward the things that his companion loved.

The wife's mother, who lived in the home with them and who was also a godly Christian, frequently joined the daughter in prayer for her companion. Often during the day they poured out their hearts to the Lord of the harvest on his behalf. They did not know how the Holy Spirit would work, but they looked to Him with expectation month after month and year after year, apparently in vain.

The Spirit does not always work as quickly as we would like, nor in the ways that we plan, for "His ways are not our ways." Our friend would return from his work, day after day, unchanged and unmoved. He opposed any Christian work on the part of his wife, would not permit her to give her money or her time to any Christian enterprise. He would not accompany her to the services. Christians were not invited to the home, nor would they be welcome if they came.

It seemed to the wife that the more she prayed, the harder he became. Nothing seemed to soften his heart or change his attitude. He seemed to be confirmed in his worldliness and established in his animosities. Other Christians were asked to pray for him and frequently did so. He avoided meeting Christians on the street, and if any should come to the home to visit, he would conveniently absent himself, lest they should talk to him about his soul.

The friend of whom we are writing was about thirty-three years of age—a fine, tall, stalwart man. He had a good position, made fairly good wages, and took good care of his home in a financial way. In most ways he was an ideal husband. His only fault was in his attitude toward the Lord and the things of God.

One evening, some friends requested Mr. P——— to go with them for a ride out in the country, where some business was to be transacted. These men took a few drinks of liquor after they were outside the city limits, and as a result, the driver lost control of the car and went into a ditch. Fortunately no one was injured, but through this narrow escape from death, the husband began to think of his eternal welfare. He had never before been near death. This new experience disturbed his peace of mind. The prayers of the wife and her mother were being answered in part.

When Mr. P——— returned home and told the story of the accident, there was much thanksgiving to God on the part of those who loved him, because God had preserved him from death and eternal punishment. Mrs. P——— had not thought of this peculiar way in which the Holy Spirit might work in dealing with her companion. She could readily see, however, that this sudden wreck had caused the husband to think along the very lines about which she had been praying. She had asked the Lord to make him look at life and death more seriously and to cause eternal things to become more real to him.

The next day, the husband returned to his work and continued for several days as though nothing had happened. Meanwhile, the two faithful ones at home continued to ask the Lord to deepen the work in his heart and to finish what He had begun. Shortly thereafter, another automobile trip was taken, this time accompanied by a gentlemen and his wife. Mr. and Mrs. P——— occupied the rear seat of the car. As they were hurrying along the highway, another car suddenly turned in from a side road, and a collision was inevitable. The two cars did not collide broadside, but the glancing blow was sufficient to overturn the car in which all four were riding. This trip had been preceded by a prayer for their preservation. The Holy Spirit heard the cry and graciously saved them from physical injury. Again, a prayer of thanksgiving arose to God for the wonderful way in which He had preserved them from injury and death.

Returning home, Mrs. P——— reminded her husband again of the dangers besetting his path, and the doom that would await him if he should die unsaved. He did not reply with his usual bitterness, nor his accustomed sneer at the things of God. It could be seen that he was somewhat worried and that the two accidents had solemnized his thinking and aroused his fears. During the day, earnest prayer was made to God that no accident would fatally injure him and that Satan would not nullify the effects already produced.

Several weeks passed with no apparent change in the attitude and decision of Mr. P———. As Thanksgiving Day approached, it was planned by the family that they, together with another group, would go for a picnic out in the woods. Although there was a Bible conference that day which the wife and mother desired very much to attend, they thought it wise to go with the husband, hoping that in the quiet of the countryside they might have an opportunity of winning him for Christ. The journey was made without mishap, and the day was filled with pleasantries of many

kinds. They remained during the evening, for the weather
was balmy and the fields were very inviting, and returned
quite late at night.

As the group rode along at a rather rapid pace, suddenly
there loomed up in front of the car a truck stalled on the
road and without lights. The sudden danger frightened the
occupants of the car and the driver attempted in vain to
swerve his car sufficiently to miss the truck, but he failed.
One of the front wheels struck the rear of the truck, over-
turning the car. One was killed and two were injured, but
Mr. and Mrs. P———— with the mother escaped uninjured.
This tragedy was the final blow to the indifference of our
friend.

The surviving ones hastened to obtain help, and after
doing all that could be done, they came directly to my home.
It was past midnight, and I was just retiring after some late
visits, but I hastened to the door. Mr. P———— stood there
trembling and very nervous. I invited him at once to enter
and be seated in my office. He recounted to me the story
of his three accidents. "I want to be saved," he said. "You
know how I have avoided you for years and did not want
either your presence or your message. Now I want to be
saved. My wife and mother have often prayed for me, and
I know you have. I have acted very foolishly, but now God
has been warning me, and I want to become a Christian.
The hour is late, but will you take time to tell me?"

It was with great joy that I took the Word of God
and opened it to help this seeker. We first read together
1 Timothy 1:15: " 'This is a faithful saying, and worthy of
all acceptation, that Christ Jesus came into the world to save
sinners.' We may be certain of this," I said, "that God sent
Christ to save you, and that Jesus came with the express
purpose of saving you. You do not need to wonder whether
He will. You may *know* that He will. You do not need to
question His desire; His coming proves that desire. Would
you like Him to save you now?"

"That is what I came to you for tonight, Doctor," he
said. "I do want Jesus to save me tonight if He will."

The next Scripture which we read was Isaiah 53:5: "But he was wounded for our transgressions, he was bruised for our iniquities: the chastisement of our peace was upon him; and with his stripes we are healed." It seemed to be a new thought to this man that Christ had been punished for him. The Scripture was very plain, and he seemed to grasp it readily. The Holy Spirit had already convicted him of his need, had revealed his future doom to him, and was now bringing before him the work of the Lord Jesus on the Cross as a substitute for him. In the car outside, in front of the house, the wife and mother were earnestly praying for his conversion to God through the Lord Jesus Christ.

"How do I know," said he, "that Jesus really was dying for me? I want to be sure that He was."

"Did we not just read that Christ came to save sinners? Let us read it again in Romans 5:6: 'For when we were yet without strength, in due time Christ died for the ungodly.'"

"That Scripture must apply to me," he said, "for I feel so helpless and utterly hopeless. I cannot see why God should want to save me now, after these years of rebellion and my attitude of hatred toward Him. Are you sure that it refers to me?"

"Yes, I am quite sure," I replied, "for the Lord Jesus Himself said, 'All that the Father giveth me shall come to me; and him that cometh to me I will in no wise cast out' (John 6:37). Notice also, Mr. P————, John 1:12: 'But as many as received him, to them gave he power to become the sons of God, even to them that believe on his name.'" I assured him that Jesus Christ is now on the throne waiting to receive him as a sinner and ready to save his soul if he would only trust Him to do it.

"I will gladly trust Him right now," said he; and kneeling beside the desk, he committed his soul to Christ Jesus the Lord and received Him with his whole heart. Peace at once enveloped his soul, and tears of joy filled his eyes. He thanked the Saviour for dying for him. Mr. P———— soon made his way to the door and thence to the automobile, where his wife and mother were waiting, pleading, and watching.

There was a wonderful reunion out there in the darkness of the night. The light of the Lord, however, filled their hearts, and they went home rejoicing. Mr. P———— is now serving the Lord among the people of God and telling the story of salvation to all that he may meet.

I Went Halfway with God

In a summer conference in the South, held especially for the benefit of young people, there was a little lad about twelve years of age who had come about two hundred miles for the ten-day Bible class. He was a very earnest little fellow. He attended Sunday school regularly in the city from which he came and liked very much to be around Christian people. He had a religious nature and was interested in religious things, even though so young.

My attention had been directed to him during the services because he usually sat on the front seat and paid very close attention to all that was said. He always had a hymn book and sang lustily, as though he really enjoyed it.

It was a time of heart-searching at this conference. Because there were so many young people there, the ministry was rather simple, pointed, and plain. Personal conferences were held between the services so that the young people might ask questions concerning their own individual needs and problems. This lad was of an inquiring mind and asked many questions about the things he heard from the platform which were not clearly understood. He was not a careless listener but an earnest one, desiring to let nothing escape his attention.

During the ten days a number of his companions had trusted the Saviour and found a new peace such as he did not possess. Because of their age and lack of experience, these who had trusted Christ could only say in their simplicity,

"I trusted the Lord Jesus, and He saved me, and now I have peace in my heart." This short, terse testimony, of course, did not bring very much light to the heart of our little friend, Henry Laird. He was not satisfied at all with something that he could not understand, and neither would he drift along in the dark without making an effort to obtain the information his heart desired.

Little Henry grew more and more troubled about his soul as the meetings progressed and as he saw others finding the peace and joy that he wanted. One night he came to the service and, as usual, sat in the front row, singing heartily in every song and quite oblivious of the other young people around him.

The message was about God's gift to men—the gift of Christ. John 1:12 was used as a text, and also John 3:16. I sought to stress in the message that salvation is not some article which may be picked up at random; it is not like a piece of fruit on the tree which may be plucked when desired. Salvation is a Person. When Simeon took the baby Jesus up in his arms, he said, "Mine eyes have seen Thy salvation" (Luke 2:30). When Jesus entered the home of Zacchaeus, He said, "This day is salvation come to this house" (Luke 19:9). God said about Christ, "I will also give thee for a light to the Gentiles, that thou mayest be my salvation unto the end of the earth" (Isa. 49:6; Acts 13:47).

I endeavored to show the children that salvation is not a feeling or a peculiar experience that takes place when they have done some special act. It was my plan and purpose to present the Lord Jesus to them in such a way that they would see that He Himself is the Saviour. It is not His work that saves; it is He who saves. It is not believing in His works that brings peace; it is accepting His Person and believing in Him who has done the sufficient work at Calvary.

The Lord stirred the hearts of many that evening, and they were examining their hearts to see whether they had really received the gift of the Lord Jesus Christ from the loving hand of God or whether they had simply had a religious experience without taking Christ. Several trusted the

Lord Jesus that evening, but little Henry did not make a confession. I could see that there was a cloud on his face, for he did not clearly understand the message as I had given it. We must remember that the darkened mind does not grasp quickly the Light of life. The Holy Spirit must do that wonderful work. He must illuminate the soul. He must deliver from tradition and darkness. He must shine into the dark heart and dispel the doubts and disperse the fears. Only He can do it!

The after-meeting lasted for some little time because a number of these precious young folks asked for help and guidance. Several Christian workers were busy answering the questions, some of which were strange and unusual. Let us never be in a hurry to urge a heart to make a confession. When the Light comes, a confession is automatic. When the soul really sees the Truth, the darkness is gone, and faith fills the heart with peace.

I was sorry to see my little lad go away without Christ. I had hoped and prayed that the message would be so clear and simple that he would be delivered from the chains of darkness that were around his little heart, and I really had expected that, because of his deep interest, he would be one of the first to announce his trust in Christ Jesus. As he left the service, I prayed for him, asking the blessed Lord of the harvest to gather in this little "grain of wheat" for His glory.

That evening, although other children gathered around the front of the hotel to talk about the service and to help each other, Henry was nowhere to be seen. A number of us who were especially interested in him were praying that he was away with the Lord and his Bible, seeking the solution of his perplexity. This was exactly the case. He had gone away to his bed in the dormitory and taken advantage of the quiet there while the other boys were out in the yard enjoying the evening and the company. There he put his finger on the passage 1 John 5:12, "He that hath the Son hath life," and said to his Lord, "Lord Jesus, I take you tonight as my Saviour, and I will be all yours from now on." It was not a long, weary, laborious, dry prayer. His heart was in it, his soul was poured out to the Saviour, and the Holy Spirit revealed Christ to his heart.

We did not know of this transaction the next day. Evidently Henry was not quite sure that he was really saved. He meditated on the Scriptures during the day, listened to the afternoon message, listened to the Christians talking together around the grounds, but did not tell us what had transpired in his heart.

The time for the evening service arrived, and to our great joy Henry was sitting on the front seat again with his hymnbook and a Bible.

The sermon was about "Believing God." The illustration was used of Abraham ready to offer up Isaac and of the dying thief trusting in a dying Saviour who was dying more rapidly than himself. I told of Peter, willing to step out of the boat on the water; and of the woman, willing to set out vessels for the oil; and of the soldiers, who dug the ditch for water when there was none in sight. Of course, after each illustration, an appeal was made for the soul to trust the Lord Jesus without reservation or hesitation.

Henry listened most attentively, sometimes watching the preacher and sometimes with his head bowed in meditation on what he was hearing. At the end of the service we did not give a call for any to come forward and make a confession, but the service was turned into a testimony meeting during which we hoped and expected that some would for the first time rise where they were and acknowledge their faith in the Lord Jesus.

The testimonies began immediately. One after another told how he had been directed to the conference by a hungering heart and had found the Saviour there. Others told how their faith had been strengthened by the truths that were presented. Still others told how they had drifted and wandered and now at this series of meetings had been brought back to a new walk with their Lord.

Our hearts kept praying for Henry, for we were especially drawn to him because of his earnest, simple hunger for the truth. As we were looking to God for him, and at the same time listening to the testimonies, suddenly he arose and, with a clear, shrill voice, almost cried out, "Folks, last year I went to a revival meeting and sort of went halfway with God. I've been listening to these sermons, and tonight I want to tell all of you that I'm going all the way with God." His little heart could not express more, and he sat down weeping for joy. One of the Christian friends hurried to his side and put an arm about him affectionately and with open Bible helped him to see in a new way and more fully all that the Lord Jesus had done for him and all that the Saviour would be to him. His was a happy heart that evening as the new faith filled his face with a new light and put a new song in his heart.

During the few days of the conference that remained, we were happy to see that Henry Laird had really had a meeting with the Lord Jesus and had experienced the freedom and the radiant hope to which the faith of his little heart entitled him.

Reader, you too may go "all the way with God." Accept the Lord Jesus right now, and He will cleanse you from your sins in His precious blood.

The Atheist Doctor

It seems both strange and sad that so many of our fine physicians do not believe in our Lord Jesus Christ. They do their work well. They are kind to the afflicted. They spend their lives in the service of others. They will go at any hour of the day or night where duty calls. They realize the seriousness and the danger of death and yet make no provision for the safety of the soul who dies. They make no provision for their own souls. This story will relate to you the blessing that came to one such physician who was practicing medicine in a small town in Kansas.

Dr. White had graduated from a medical college in which there was a very fine Christian physician who gave lectures to the students. This professor's faith and his godly life had attracted and won the admiration of the young student. He had often said that this Christian doctor was his favorite teacher. In addition to being a good Christian, the professor was an excellent teacher and was thoroughly versed in his subject of medicines, their character, and their uses. He was able to impart his information to the students in such a way that they were able to retain the instructions.

The young medical student was not interested at all in Christianity; in fact, he was quite opposed to Christian doctrines and principles. The real reason for his opposition lay in the fact that he loved his sins and did not want Christianity to hinder his free and easy way of living. Rather

than get rid of his sins, he tried to blot out Christianity, thinking
that thereby his conscience would be eased, and he could
live as he pleased. He remained away from gospel services,
ignored the Bible, and made a mockery of Christian things.
It was my good fortune to be called to this little city
where Dr. White lived to hold a series of meetings in the
Presbyterian church. As is usually my custom, I inquired of
the pastor concerning the spiritual life of the physicians of
the town. He informed me that some of them were friendly
to the church and would sometimes attend the services. Others
were not at all friendly and remained away constantly from
services of every kind. He particularly mentioned the antagonism of Dr. White. He made known his atheistic doctrines and theories to his patients and rather gloated over
the victories he had won in private debates with Christians.
He was aggressive in his unbelief and active in propagating
his wicked theories.

The doctor should be a believer. He sees the miracles
of the human body. He sees the wonderful workings of mental
processes. He sees the tragedy of dying in the dark. He ob-
serves the cruel ravages of sin which wreck the human body.
He should realize, above all others, that Christ Jesus alone
can transform the heart and implant in the soul a love for
righteousness and a hatred of sin. He knows very well that
all he can do is for the body, and after that he can do no
more. He sees the death of the saint, where peace and rest
abound and comfort fills the heart. He sees the death of the
wicked, where fear, dread, and hopelessness pervade the whole
soul and heart of the patient. All of this should stir his heart
to want to be a real Christian.

Having heard of the attitude of Dr. White, I presented
myself at his office and requested an interview. This he readily
granted. He took me into his private office, and, as I entered
the door, I was delightfully surprised to see, hanging on the
wall, a framed picture of the Christian professor he had so
much liked while in college. I said to him, "Oh, I see you
have Dr. Wilson's picture hanging on your wall. Did you
like him, and did you enjoy his classes?"

He replied with some joy, "Yes, Dr. Wilson was my favorite professor. He was a sane and sensible Christian and was able to tell what he knew in a way that made me remember it."

"I am glad to know this," I said, "because he was my father. It is a joy to me to hear one of his students speak well of him." Up until now, the doctor had been somewhat formal and stiff in his attitude toward me, but now his whole demeanor changed.

"You cannot know how glad I am to meet you," he said with much joy. "I consider it an honor to know a son of Dr. Wilson, whom I esteemed so highly, and I certainly am happy to have you call on me. Are you the preacher who is preaching over at the Presbyterian church?"

"Yes," I answered, "and I came over today to ask whether you cannot spare a little time to attend the service. I believe you would enjoy it."

The doctor became quite friendly now, as he invited me to be seated opposite his desk where he took his place in his office chair. "Dr. Wilson," he began, "your father tried to talk to me about religion, but I never could see anything in it. I am an atheist. I do not believe that the Bible is true, nor do I believe in a God. Sometimes I wish it were not so and that I could really believe what you Christians believe."

This frank response pleased me. I saw that through the years, troubles of various kinds had made him more thoughtful and more considerate. To me this was a good sign. It indicated that God was working in this man's heart and that perhaps he would not be so difficult to reach as the pastor had thought. Sometimes we place men in positions of antagonism and opposition in which they really should not be placed. Oftentimes we shall find that those who seem to be hard and difficult to reach are not quite so antagonistic as we thought. Let us approach every friend whom we would win for Christ with kindness and courtesy.

"Tell me, Doctor, what it is in the Bible that you do not believe. There are many things there that you must admit are true and accurate. Perhaps you just refer to certain things that are not pleasing to you and which you hope are not true. Is that correct?"

Those who make the broad statement that the Bible is not true should always be given an opportunity to tell just what things the Bible says which they know positively to be untrue. This will pin the friend down to specific facts and will probably take the foundation from under his feet. It was so in this case.

The doctor replied to me, "I do not know any of it that I believe. It seems to me to be just a lot of fables and oriental stories with the colorings of the civilizations of that time."

I continued my question by asking, "Do you refer, Doctor, to things that the Bible says about ants, trees, gravitation, and precipitation? Do you think that what the Scripture records about the rise and fall of certain kingdoms is not true?

"Do you also question the veracity of the statements in the Bible about birds and their nests, sheep and their lambs, the evil results of sin in the human life? Do you believe that the Bible gives incorrect instructions when it says that the husbands should love their wives, and that the children should obey their parents, and that kings should rule in righteousness and equity? I can hardly believe, Doctor, that you deny these basic principles."

His answer was not long in coming. "Oh, no, I believe all of that. I do not know a better code of ethics or standard of morals than that which the Bible gives."

"Thank you, Doctor," I said, "this relieves my mind considerably, for now I see that you are a believer in part, and that you do admit that some parts of the Bible are quite true and dependable. Tell me, Doctor, just exactly what thing in the Bible you feel is untrue and inaccurate."

He answered at once, "I do not believe in a God who would punish anybody. The Bible says that God will put people in hell and burn them forever. That idea is repulsive to me, and I do not want anything to do with a God of that character."

"Doctor, what would you do with the vile, filthy people of earth? Would you expect to find all the people in eternity enjoying the same blessings and privileges? Would it be in your mind that if there is a God, He should overlook all the sins and wickednesses of men and take them all into His own great home to live with Him as His companions? Do you think that this would be right?"

"Certainly not," he said, "that would not be right at all, but I do not believe that they should be punished in hell." The doctor was becoming more earnest by this time. He was meditating more carefully, and I could see that my kindly and logical answer or question was causing him to do some very serious thinking.

"Doctor, what would be your idea of what God should do with vile sinners?"

He answered, "I think that there should be degrees of reformation after death, but I cannot see this eternal burning business."

I saw that the doctor was not as firmly fixed in his convictions as some had thought he was, and I felt happy to continue my conversation; but as I began to do so, a patient entered the front office, and the doctor said to me hurriedly, "When can I see you again?"

I answered him by saying, "Tonight I will preach at the church on the subject 'Will a Good God Punish Wicked Sinners?' This sermon will be exactly what you want, and I believe it will help you." He promised to come and said he would lay aside everything else to come and hear the son of his old favorite professor.

As I sat on the platform in the church building, I watched the door eagerly, waiting for the coming of Dr. White. As the second song was given out, he entered the auditorium and took a seat near the back. The pastor and I had agreed that we would pray for this friend and look to the Holy Spirit to bring the light into his dark heart. In my message that evening I called attention to the fact that God would judge the sinner and would punish him according to His own estimate of that sinner's sin. Man judges and condemns according to man's estimate. Man would like to make God judge and punish the sinner according to man's estimate of the guilt.

One of the illustrations used struck home to the heart of the doctor, and I watched his countenance as it took on a decided change in expression as I told the story of a little girl. The story was as follows: "Suppose, my friend, that you should tell me that you have a lovely little girl ten years of age with beautiful brown eyes and lovely, attractive, brown curls. She is your only daughter, and you love her deeply and devotedly. As you come home from your work some evening and pass along the walk that leads down to your house, sitting back in the woods, you hear a loud scream of agony and fear with other screams of fright and of terrible pain. The voice sounds like the voice of your beautiful little sweetheart. You drop your packages and run as quickly as possible to the clump of bushes from which the sounds emanate. There you find a brutish fiend choking, beating, and assaulting that lovely little body. He is injuring her terribly and treating her with cruel beatings. What would you do now to reveal your heart of love and to prove to us that you are a kind, devoted, loving father?" At this point in the story I hesitated a few moments in order that the audience might fully realize the seriousness of the scene and the mental processes of that father. I was particularly interested in the face of my doctor friend.

The story had gripped the audience; the answer was quite evident. I continued by saying, "Would you not at once attack this human monster and with the greatest force subdue him? Would you not deliver him to the officers of the law in order that he might be properly and severely punished? Perhaps your own hatred and vengeance would completely wreck the brute, and you would leave him lifeless on the ground while you hurried with your baby to the nearest hospital. You would do all of this as a proof of your love for the treasure of your home, the little girl. The severe treatment you would give her assailant would be the measure of your love for your daughter. Let me ask you, my friend,

what, in your judgment, should God do with those who hate
His Son, revile Him, mock Him, cast Him out, and participate
in His crucifixion? God's own answer is 'He that believeth
not the Son shall not see life, but the wrath of God abideth
on Him' " (John 3:36).

I could see that the doctor had made a decision in his
heart. His question was answered. A good God, who loves
His Son, *will* punish the enemies of His Son. Those who
follow Satan, who is the archenemy of Jesus Christ, must
suffer the vengeance of an angry God. I went to the doctor's
office the next morning and found him a believer. He had
seen that the logic of his reasoning was all wrong. He had
accepted God's estimate of sin, had believed in the righteousness of God, and had accepted the gift of His Son, Jesus
Christ. I left him with that beautiful passage, 1 John 5:12,
"He that hath the Son hath life, and he that hath not the
Son of God hath not life."

God can never use or bless anyone who argues with
Him, nor will He save anyone who disagrees with Him.
"Abraham believed God, and it was counted unto him for
righteousness." So may you.

The Case of the Japanese Barber

All morning long, I had sought time and opportunity to shave myself before starting on a trip to Los Angeles from the neighboring village in which I was visiting. One circumstance after another combined to prevent this, until it was time to leave for the city. Hurrying up the long road to the interurban station, I went to the ticket window to purchase a ticket to the city, and there the agent told me that the electric train was two hours late.

I felt that the Holy Spirit had some special work for me to do, else I would not have been hindered from shaving in the home of my host. I surmised that somewhere He had a barber to whom I was to have the privilege of giving the gospel that day.

Upon learning the train was late, I started walking down the street, seeking a barber shop, at the same time looking to the Lord to guide and direct me aright. Two blocks down the street was a small revolving sign which attracted me, and I approached the shop. As I opened the door, a bell rang, arousing the barber who was then in the rear of the shop, behind a partition.

We met near the barber chair, and I observed that he was a Japanese, a young man of about thirty-five. I asked for a shave, and he politely requested me to sit in the chair, which I did. Adjusting the chair to a reclining position, he soon had the warm lather on my face, with a hot towel to soften the beard. While he sharpened his razor, I asked the Holy Spirit for wisdom to approach this man in a wise way, so that I might win him for Christ.

I inquired of him whether he knew a Mr. Kimura, who is called the "Billy Sunday" of Japan.

"Where is he from?" he asked.

"His home is in Kioto, but he preaches all over Japan."

"Oh, I came from Kioto. I was born there," he said. "Is this Mr. Kimura a little man who builds big, wooden tabernacles, with sawdust on the ground?"

"Yes," I said, "that is his method."

My answer produced a deep impression. He obtained a clean towel, wiped the lather from my face until it was dry, raised the chair in order that I might assume a sitting posture, then leaning over the chair, with solemn countenance and a serious voice, he said, "I will never forget that little man. I went to one of his meetings in Kioto and heard him preach. When he finished, he came from the platform down the aisle, placed his hand on my shoulder, and said, 'Young man, how are you going to get rid of your sins?' "

"Have you found out how?" I asked at once.

"No," he answered. "I wish I could. When you rang the bell, I was walking up and down in my little room at the back of the shop, saying those words over and over again and wishing that I knew. Can you tell me?"

"Yes, indeed, I can," said I, whereupon I arose from the chair, obtained my Bible, and returned to read to him the story of the Saviour's love.

Acts 10:43 impressed his heart very much: "To him give all the prophets witness, that through his name whosoever believeth in him shall receive remission of sins." Another Scripture was read, Colossians 2:14: "Blotting out the handwriting of ordinances that was against us, which was contrary to us, and took it out of the way, nailing it to his cross."

"Have you any sins?" I asked.

"Oh, yes," he answered, "lots of them."

"Would you like to have them put away today?"

"If it could be so," he eagerly answered, "I would get peace in my heart, for now only trouble is there."

"Well, Jesus came to blot out your sins for you. I will read it for you in Isaiah 44:22: 'I have blotted out, as a thick cloud, thy transgressions, and, as a cloud, thy sins: return unto me; for I have redeemed thee.'"

These passages seemed to affect deeply the heart of the barber, but still he did not have peace. He seemed in deep meditation as I explained the Scriptures to him and told him about the Saviour of sinners who came to save him. I then turned to 1 John 1:7: "The blood of Jesus Christ his Son cleanseth us from all sin." I explained it to him, saying, "Do you not see, Mr. Barber, that the Lord Jesus was dying for you? He suffered on the Cross the punishment that you should have had." We then read Romans 5:6: "When we were yet without strength, in due time Christ died for the ungodly."

These Scriptures brought the light to his dark and troubled soul. The peace of God came into his heart as he confessed his belief in the work of Christ at Calvary and his acceptance of the person of Christ for his own soul. "Jesus put my sins away," he said. "The Bible says so. I believe the Bible. I believe God sent Jesus to save me, and I take Him. He is mine." These were the expressions from the heart of this man who had first met the Saviour and received the gift of a new and eternal life.

I then said to him, "Did none of your customers ever tell you of the Saviour?"

"No," he replied, "they do not talk about Jesus to me."

"Have you not been to any of our American churches?"

"Yes," he said, "but they did not tell me that Jesus blotted out my sins for me and that I could have Him as my own Saviour. No one seemed to care whether I was saved or not. It was mostly religion and singing and talking about many things, but I could not find peace in what they said. I am so glad you have come with your Bible to show me how to get rid of my sins."

Before continuing with the shaving, I said, "Are your sins gone now? Are they blotted out?"

"Yes," he replied, "Jesus has put them away, and I believe in Him."

The shave I received that day will never be surpassed. How carefully he handled the razor and me! How kind he was and how grateful! I left him with joy and peace, for his sins had been blotted out.

There Are Two Kinds of Waitresses

It was my privilege to take lunch one day with a prominent businessman who was interested in the church where I was holding services. He had requested that I go with him for this luncheon engagement in order that we might talk together about the work of the church, and particularly about certain individuals whom we were seeking to help in spiritual matters.

His chauffeur was instructed to drive us down to a celebrated restaurant in the heart of the city and, after leaving us there, to return in two hours to take us back to the church for the afternoon service.

We were soon seated at a table in the beautiful dining room where luxury prevailed. Many were dining in this well-known restaurant, and the waitresses, nicely dressed in white, were busy serving here and there. We sat for some time waiting for one of these friends to serve us.

After a while there came an attractive young lady to the table, and, with a smile and a word of greeting, she placed a glass of water before each of us and laid down a menu card. She then waited with pencil and pad in her hand until we should order our meal.

The kind attitude of this waitress and her evident desire to serve kindly and faithfully made it easy for me to speak to her, which I did by saying, "My friend, do you know that there are two kinds of waitresses?"

She leaned over smiling and said, "No, are there? Oh, yes, perhaps there are, for there are good ones and bad ones."

"No," I replied, "that is not the distinction. It is true
that there are good ones and bad ones, but it is also true
that there are saved ones and lost ones." Looking full into
her face for a moment, I said, "Tell me, young lady, which
kind are you?"

No doubt, it had been many days since such a question
was presented to this lady's heart. She was a bit startled at
first and then amused. Then she became thoughtful, the smile
disappeared, and she said rather seriously, "You know, mister, that is one of the troubles with this job. I must serve
just the same on Sunday as on every other day, and I cannot
go to church. I used to go to Sunday school before I began
working downtown, but you know how easy it is to get
engrossed in the work, and especially when the hours are
such that to attend church is out of the question."

I was glad to see this happy and thoughtful response
to my inquiry. She did not throw my question away with
an utter disregard. She rather welcomed it. Her case is not
at all uncommon, for there are thousands of lovely young
people who, because of the necessities of life, are forced to
serve on Sunday as well as evenings and are thereby deprived
of the privilege and opportunity of assembling with Christians
in the service of the Lord.

My friend sitting opposite me at the table was himself
an able soulwinner with a heart intent on winning men to
Christ. While I was talking with the young lady, he had
taken from his pocket a copy of the Gospel of John, and
he said, "Here, young lady, you will find in this Gospel of
John God's message of life to you and His provision of
salvation for you. You may not get to church, but you may
read this message from the Lord to your heart any time and
anywhere. Do let me urge you to do so."

She accepted the gift of the Gospel with a very happy
little "thank you" and seemed glad to obtain it.

Our new friend hastened away to the kitchen and after
some little time returned with our meal, which she carefully
placed before us, arranging the silverware and the dishes in
proper order.

As she was doing so, I continued my conversation by saying, "Are you a lost girl? I do not believe you answered that question a while ago when I inquired."

She gave a little toss of her head in a rather careless manner and said, "I suppose I am, for I certainly am not a Christian."

The answer pleased me, and I immediately replied, "You may be a saved girl today if you would like, right in the dining room and right here beside the table. It is not necessary for you to go to church to be saved. You may find the Lord Jesus here and now, if your heart is ready and your mind so desires."

The thought of being saved in the dining room, and so quickly, rather shocked the waitress, and she looked at me in amazement. She looked also at my friend. He smiled and nodded his head to give approval to what I was saying, and this encouraged her to believe that perhaps there was something to it. "How can that be?" she inquired. "I thought you had to go to church and go down to the front and have a talk with the preacher, and someway or other something would happen."

I assured her that such was not the case and that the Lord Jesus would save her gladly and immediately if she would come to Him in trusting faith.

By this time I had taken my Bible from my pocket and read to her, "He that hath the Son hath life; and he that hath not the Son of God hath not life" (1 John 5:12). "You see, little lady," I continued, "salvation is found only in the Lord Jesus. When you commit your cause and your case to Him and trust your soul to Him, you are safe in His hands, and He will do everything that is necessary to save you, to redeem you, and to deliver you. Why not let Him do it? He loves you dearly. He gave His life as a sacrifice for you, and I am sure that you have heard all about this long ago."

She assured me that she had often heard the Bible preached when she was a little girl but had forgotten most of it. She did agree with me, however, that the Lord Jesus is the Saviour and that no one else can save the soul but He.

Having finished her work in placing the meal properly before us, she left us again while we ate. We prayed together for her salvation and looked to the Holy Spirit to do a blessed work in her heart, so that when she would return with our dessert, she would be ready to take the Saviour.

It was as we had prayed. She did return after a while, cleared away the dishes, removed the soiled silver, and then brought the dessert. As she placed it on the table, I said to her, "Do you not see that the Lord Jesus bore your sins at Calvary and came to be your own Saviour? Why not trust Him just now and make Him altogether your own?"

"I have been thinking quite seriously about it, sir," she answered, "since you first spoke to me a while ago. I did not know that I could become a Christian here, but since you assure me that I may accept Christ anywhere, I am willing to take Him now, and I trust Him to save me now."

My friend said to her, "You will now read the little book with a new joy, I know, for now you will understand much of what you are reading. You will find that this new life which has been given you by the Lord Jesus today will crave more and more of this precious Book. I commend you to a loving walk with the Saviour and to much knowledge of Him, which I know you will gain through reading this Gospel."

With a "good-bye" and "God bless you," we left and trust that our blessed Lord is taking care of that new-born lamb.

My friend, be sure that you do not use as an excuse your busy life or the demands of your business or any other thing which will keep you from trusting Jesus and becoming a child of God.

Saved in a Submarine

Who would ever think that a man could be saved at the bottom of the ocean, sitting in comfort on the sandy bottom of the sea?

Two sailor boys passed through our city on the way to Long Beach to join the fleet. They had been on furlough and had a few hours' wait between trains here. One was a Christian boy who knew the Lord but was not very active in his witness and testimony. He had a heart that responded to God's things but did not promote very much Christian activity in his own life. His pal was a splendid young fellow who made a good companion in the training camps. These two were wandering about on one of the main streets of our city seeing the sights. They were complete strangers here and had no friends and no acquaintances.

On Sunday afternoon two of our young people from the church were visiting various hotels in the business section of the city to leave invitations with the desk clerk asking guests to come to the meetings out at our church. They saw these sailor boys in uniform and gave each of them an invitation, accompanied by a card that told the location of the church and the hour of the meetings.

Since the train on which they were to leave did not depart until about 10:00 P.M., and since the church was only a few minutes' ride from the railroad station, they decided to attend the service that night. They came in uniform and,

of course, received a very cordial welcome, especially from
the young people's group. They were made to feel at home
and soon found themselves among friends. One of our young
ladies gave to the Christian boy a copy of my book *The
Romance of a Doctor's Visits*. I do not know why the unsaved
boy did not receive a book. The Christian lad took it with
him, intending to read it on the train. Somehow he placed
it in one of his bags and then forgot it.

When the two sailor boys arrived at Long Beach, they
found that the submarine on which they were stationed was
to leave that night. They hurriedly completed any prepara-
tions that needed to be made and boarded the ship. The
book still remained unnoticed and unread. Sometime during
the night the submarine quietly slipped away for a trip to
Japan. It was to be stationed on one of the shipping lanes
off the coast of Japan where they were to await the opportunity
to torpedo a Japanese ship.

While the submarine was resting on the ocean bed, our
Christian friend suddenly remembered the book he had
received in the young people's meeting while he was en route
to California. He searched through his baggage and found
the book. He read it with delight and was refreshed in his
own spirit by the messages he found there. Having finished
it, he gave it to his buddy with the recommendation that
he read it carefully and with the promise that he would enjoy
it. The hours passed in the submarine were a bit dreary,
and so the sailor boy was glad to get the book and began
to read it. The stories intrigued him. He began to realize
that some of the cases mentioned there were just like his
own. Before he had gone very far in his reading, he began
to realize that he too was a lost man, needing a Saviour.
The Spirit of God reminded him that he was in a war and
might never come out alive. As this truth took hold of his
heart, he watched more eagerly for the remedy.

In each of the stories that he read, he found that Christ
Jesus and the seeking sinner came together, with the blessed
result that the seeker found the Saviour to be sufficient. He
read, "Come unto me, all ye that labor and are heavy laden,

and I will give you rest." In another case, he read, "He that hath the Son hath life." In the story about an aged sinner, he read in John 3:16 that he was to take the Saviour as God's gift to him; then in John 1:12 he read that he would become a child of God by taking the Saviour; also in 1 John 5:12, he read, "He that hath the Son hath life." This was sufficient for his heart. He bowed his head to his Saviour and accepted Him as the Lord of his life and the Saviour of his soul.

He finished reading the book, where the various messages confirmed his faith, and returned it to his pal, saying, "I will never forget your kindness in giving me that wonderful book. I found Jesus Christ while I was reading it. I believe He gave me eternal life and I am His. Now we are brothers as well as pals."

How blessed it is to find that there is a welcome from the Saviour, whether we come to him in the parlor, or in the office, or in the church, or in the depths of the sea. "This Man receiveth sinners" anywhere, any place, any time.

The Ticket Did Not Arrive on Time

Having been confined to my bed for a number of months because of a severe illness, I was obliged to take a vacation out of doors so that I might regain my health. It was therefore planned that this rest period should be in California, hoping that the warm days, the new surroundings, and the healthful atmosphere would contribute materially toward a rapid recovery to normal health and strength.

About the time of this decision, a letter came from a friend in an eastern city, whom I had befriended some years prior to this occasion when he was in deep distress. In this letter my friend confided that he had never felt entirely satisfied nor happy in regard to his expressions of gratitude to me in lieu of the kindness shown him at the time of his deep need. He therefore requested the privilege of sending some appropriate gift and urged me to tell him frankly what that might be.

Inasmuch as this friend was quite able to give liberally and seemed deeply desirous of doing so, I explained to him that because my health made a trip to the Pacific coast quite necessary, I would be most happy and grateful to receive from him a ticket to California, if that seemed to be his pleasure. The date given him for the contemplated trip was June 28.

On the morning of June 28, having finished my correspondence, I closed my various business matters and left the office for home, there to await the ticket which should have reached me through the mail that day. Word had been received from my friend that the ticket would be sent on time; however, it did not arrive.

The afternoon mail delivery did not bring the expected letter. This disturbed my mind somewhat, so I slipped downstairs to a little room in the corner of the coal bin which had been modestly equipped as a prayer room. Here I could get away from our four little children to talk with the Lord. The furniture in this small sanctuary consisted of a soap box and several minor pieces, together with an accumulation of old newspapers. Kneeling there, I poured out my heart to the Lord of the harvest, telling Him of my disappointment. My desire was to board the particular train that He wanted me to take and to occupy the very car in which He might have some friends with anxious and willing hearts to hear His Word.

The Lord gave me peace about the matter, for the case had been committed wholly to Him, and the Holy Spirit was trusted to take complete charge of the ticket, the train, the time of leaving, and every matter connected with the journey.

The next day's mail was equally disappointing; in fact, five days elapsed, and still no ticket came. I went often to the little, crudely improvised sanctuary in the basement, asking the Lord to reveal to me the cause of the delay, and, furthermore, what unusual thing He had in store for me on this journey. I felt as though there was something peculiar transpiring and watched daily in order to discover the good hand of the Lord and to discern His will concerning my path.

Having waited until July 3 without receiving the ticket, I went to my office purposely to purchase the ticket myself, being fully convinced that my friend had failed to make good his promise. While sitting in the office, meditating over the experiences of the past few days, a special-delivery letter came containing my ticket. Immediately my heart pulsated in deep gratitude to God for His kindness in sending the ticket, even though He had not yet revealed to me by His Spirit the reason for the delay.

On my way home, I purchased some fireworks for the children, in order that they might celebrate the Fourth of July, and at the supper table I informed the family that I planned to leave that evening for California. The children immediately formed a committee of protest, demanding a picnic such as they had enjoyed in previous years, and suggested that it was hardly fair for Father to take a long vacation and leave them with none. This seemed quite reasonable on their part, and I felt it was the Lord's good pleasure that I should remain another day and share with them the joys of this annual celebration.

On the evening of the Fourth of July, I boarded the train for California. The hour was late, and the passengers in the sleeping cars had retired for the night; therefore, there was no opportunity to serve the Lord or to seek for needy souls. In the morning the train stopped in western Kansas, where breakfast was being served in the station of a small town. A number of passengers alighted to take advantage of this opportunity. However, to my disappointment, I noted that the conversation of the group gathered around the table did not savor of spiritual things, and I found no evidence of the working of the Lord in those parts.

As the train proceeded on its way, I requested the porter to bring me a writing table, upon which I placed my Bible, a concordance, and a book on prayer which I was enjoying. As I interested myself in Bible study, a lady, whom I had not previously observed in the car, approached the table. She seemed to be about fifty years of age and was dressed in deep mourning. It was quite evident that some great sorrow had overtaken her for which she sought comfort.

Quickly looking to the gracious Spirit of God for wisdom and His leading, I greeted the friend by saying, "I observe that you have had a great grief in your life, and I would like very much indeed to share the burden with you. Would you not like to sit down with me and rehearse the story of your sorrow?"

"Yes, I would," she answered, and at once seated herself at the table opposite me.

"Are you a minister?" she asked.

"Partly so," I replied. "Some of my time is spent preaching and some in other labors. I love the Scriptures, however, and would like so much to help you with your problem, if there is a burden upon your heart. Will you permit me to do so?"

With an expression of eagerness and leaning forward, she said earnestly, "I was reared without knowledge of the Bible, although surrounded by religion. Not only did I attend church daily, but I gave liberally of my means and supported every enterprise of the church, thus contributing my time and effort. My husband, a judge of some prominence in a western city, together with the children, were in hearty accord with me in my religious zeal.

"One day a neighbor presented me with a copy of the New Testament, something I had never seen before, nor had I ever read it. How interesting I found it to be! One thing that seemed particularly inspiring to me was the freedom which all the folks had who wanted to come to Jesus. They came directly to Him, with no one in between. They brought every distress to Him, as well as all of their questions. To me it was wonderful to observe how tenderly the Lord dealt with them and how quickly He forgave the sins of those who came with broken hearts.

"This unusual freedom with Christ affected me so deeply that in a few days I called on my minister and asked him whether Christ, when on earth, had a private secretary. 'No,' he replied, 'He did not.' Does He now have a private secretary? 'No,' he answered, 'He does not. Why do you ask me?' Because I want to get to Jesus myself, I said; I want to get right into His presence and hear Him forgive my sins. I want to know that He has done it Himself, like He did for the people in the Bible."

My friend then explained how she had left her pastor at the close of this conversation with him to read again the Scriptures and to seek someone who would show her the way to the Saviour. "When I saw your Bible," she continued, "I thought surely you were a minister and could tell me how to find Jesus, for I feel I must get to Him soon and receive His forgiveness."

Because of her religious experiences, I turned at once to the book of Hebrews and read of the priestly work of Jesus Christ in blotting out and putting away the sins of every one who came to Him in faith. We read in Hebrews 2:17 that "Christ made reconciliation for the sins of the people." It was her sins He came to blot out. We next read in Hebrews 7:25 that "He is able also to save them to the uttermost that come unto God by him." We read, too, in Hebrews 1:3 that "When he had by himself purged our sins, sat down." The two words "by himself" particularly impressed her.

"I never realized that before," she said. "I knew that Jesus had done some things for my salvation, but I thought that the church must do much more and that I should do a great deal." Turning my Bible around in order that she might see the passage, I asked her to read the verse for herself.

As she meditated on the blessed truth that Christ "by himself" had purged her sins, we turned to Hebrews 9:26 and found this message: "But now once in the end of the world [age] hath he appeared to put away sin by the sacrifice of himself." The light was beginning to dawn in this darkened heart. Never before had she realized what Christ had done for her. It was a new revelation to her heart that the Saviour at Calvary had actually put away her sin. Again, we turned to Hebrews 10:17 and read, "And their sins and iniquities will I remember no more."

Her troubled heart found peace at once, and, extending her hand across the table, she said with tears of joy, "I see so clearly now that my Saviour has taken my sins away, and they are gone." She closed her eyes in worship and thanked the Redeemer for His love to her.

"You did not tell me about your sorrow," I said.

"No, I did not," she replied, "and you will be surprised when I say that I am glad this sorrow came when it did.

While in Blackstone visiting my sister, I purchased my return ticket with Pullman reservations, intending to begin my journey on the night of June 26. This would have brought me through Kansas City on the night of June 28. On the twenty-sixth, my sister became quite ill with appendicitis and died on the twenty-eighth. The funeral was held on July 2, and I left that evening, which brought me through Kansas City last night. I feel deeply thankful to God that He has permitted me to be on the train that you are on with your Bible; otherwise I would have gone home unsaved and be still in my sins."

She was unaware of the gratitude and worship that surged through my soul at that same moment because of the wonderful way in which the Holy Spirit had handled this entire matter. Noticing my agitation, she asked the reason. I then told her the story of my exercise of soul concerning the trip. My plans were to leave Kansas City on the night of June 28. However, the Spirit of God, knowing she could not come through that night, caused my friend in New York to delay sending the ticket, thus hindering my departure and delaying my trip until the night of the Fourth of July. This remarkable example of the leading of the Spirit so stirred our hearts that we bowed together in reverence while I offered our united praise to God for the leading of His Spirit and the saving power of Jesus Christ.

At the conclusion of our conversation, my friend arose, walked to the rear of the car, and, as she passed from seat to seat, related to each passenger in the car the story of her wonderful conversion.

Let me remind each Christian worker that the Holy Spirit is still the Lord of the harvest. He arranges times and seasons. He brings about peculiar circumstances which work out for the salvation of men. Let us learn more and more to depend upon Him to lead us to troubled hearts and to bring together in His own peculiar way the seeking Saviour and the needy sinner.

The Dentist Took a Chance

Dr. Richards served as a dentist in a midwestern city and built up a good practice. He was honest and thorough in his work. He had a pleasing personality, made many friends, and became a deacon in the large church near his home. One day, as he journeyed on his summer's vacation, he passed through Winona Lake, Indiana, because he had heard about that great Bible conference and wanted to see what it was like. He had never been to a Bible conference, though he had read about them in the monthly magazine of his denomination. While at Winona Lake, he visited the bookstore and purchased a copy of my book *The Romance of a Doctor's Visits*. As he read the book, he found the story of a man whose condition of heart was quite like his own. The man was religious, had good standing in the community, was respected and honored as a man of the church. This man discovered that he obtained no peace in his heart from all his religious activities.

This story convinced the doctor that he too needed something else besides religion. He was a successful dentist, he was well received in society, but somehow he had no peace in his heart and no rest in his spirit. He felt the need of something more than just religious activity and good character.

He decided to lock up his office and fly to Kansas City to see the one who wrote the book and had this interesting experience about which he had read. He did so without first learning whether I would be at home and could be seen by him. Of course, the Holy Spirit is always guiding in the affairs of troubled hearts, and He knew that this seeker should not be disappointed. I was at home and received a telephone call from one of the downtown hotels to see if he could make an appointment with me that evening. We were just at supper at the time, and so I asked him to come at 7:30. He did so. He was a splendid young man about thirty-five years of age and impressed me as one who was deeply in earnest, and not just a curiosity seeker.

We sat in the parlor, and he began the conversation by saying, "I read in your book, *The Romance of a Doctor's Visits,* about a man whose case is quite like my own. I am in good standing in the city where I live. I have a splendid dental practice, and I am a deacon in the church. I have a wife and two little children whose hearts are with me in my Christian activity. In spite of all of this, I know there is something wrong with me. I get nowhere in my Christian activity and do not know for sure that I belong to the Lord. I flew over here hoping to find you, and I want you to tell me what you told that friend about whom I read in your book." I answered him by saying, "Are you a lost dentist?" He did not answer at once but was thinking the thing through. Then he said, "I do not know whether I am or not. Certainly I do not have the thing that would make me satisfied with God and give me the feeling of security."

I asked him then if he knew any verse of Scripture that he could quote. He drew a little Testament out of his pocket and without opening it said, "I learned a verse in Sunday school, and really I am ashamed to say it is the only verse I know." He then quoted correctly John 3:16, "For God so loved the world, that He gave His only begotten Son, that whosoever believeth in Him should not perish, but have everlasting life." I then reminded him that God sent the Lord Jesus to be the Saviour. He came to save from sin and to give the gift of righteousness and then eventually bring us to God after being made fit for God's presence.

He listened intently as I explained this truth to him, and then I said, "Doctor, do you realize that you are a lost man and need Christ Jesus to save you?" He answered, "That certainly is my condition. I had never heard that expression used and at first was puzzled about it. Now I see that I need someone to put away my sins and make me fit for heaven." This opened the door for the application of the gospel, so I asked him, "Is it not true that it takes two to make a gift, the one who gives and the one who takes?" "Yes," he answered, "it is true." To this I replied, "The verse you quoted tells us that God gave His Son, and God is looking for a taker. To whom did God give His Son?" My friend, the doctor, threw his head back on the big upholstered chair and, looking up to heaven, said, "God, You gave Jesus Christ to me, and I am taking Him right now. I want You to know, God, that I am trusting Your Son with my soul, and I know that He came to save me." The doctor at once entered into peace. His heart was at rest. He expressed his gratitude to God for the gift of His Son, and his gratitude to me for showing him the way.

The doctor returned to his hotel that night with a song in his heart. He and the Saviour had met together. The next morning he flew back to his home, told his wife and family about the Saviour he had found, and they had a time of rejoicing together. On Sunday he arose in the church to tell the congregation of his experience with the living Saviour who had saved his soul and had given him the peace that passeth understanding.

A few days later the doctor phoned me long distance to tell me the good news that three others in the church had found the Saviour through his testimony. He began to testify to his patients and found that Christ Jesus was really a personal Lord in his life and a living Redeemer for his soul.

She Was Not Under the Blood

Two hundred boys and girls, most of them teenagers, were gathered in the log house at the Bible camp out in the woods. They had gathered together on that beautiful summer morning to enjoy and be blessed by the morning Bible lesson before going out to play. I had chosen for my subject on that morning "How to Find the Gospel in the Old Testament." Most of these young folks had never been interested in the Old Testament. Somehow they felt that it was filled with difficult words, dry genealogies, and wars among people that they did not know. The subject was very interesting to them, and so they were waiting eagerly for the message.

This was a convention of young people from various young people's groups out of different denominations and from different parts of the state. The sponsor of each group had come with them to spend the week at this lovely lake resort. Among these sponsors was a lady about fifty-five years of age, who had brought with her seventeen teenagers; they came with their Bibles and with buoyant spirits to enjoy physical and spiritual blessings. When I was introduced to this teacher, I noticed that her Bible was well worn, which revealed that she had used it a great deal. It was "dog-eared," and many passages of Scripture had been underlined for emphasis. She sat on the front bench in this log house with her young people arranged around her.

The subject of the message on that particular morning was proving to be of great interest to the young people and to the teachers. It was a new line of thought to them, for the pictures of Christ in the Old Testament had not been pointed out to most of them. I told them the story of Cain and Abel and showed how the offering of the lamb as a substitute for the man was acceptable to God, whereas the offering of good works by Cain was not acceptable. The offering that is made for sin and for sinners must be a blood offering, and the sacrifice must die. Then I told them the story of Abraham and Isaac on Mount Moriah—how the ram caught in the bush was taken as a substitute and a sacrifice for Isaac—for again there must be the death of the sacrifice for the offerer.

As I finished telling these two stories, I noticed that my friend, the lady teacher on the front seat, was weeping. She turned her back toward me and leaned over the back of the bench on which she was sitting. I continued my explanation by using the story of the Passover Lamb, as told in Exodus 12. It is a wonderful picture of the Lord Jesus and is referred to as such in 1 Corinthians 5. I explained an imaginary case. God had instructed Moses to tell the people of Israel that every man must take a lamb, kill it, catch the blood in a basin, and sprinkle the blood on the two sides and the upper lintel of the door on the front of the house. The blood was sprinkled on the outside of the door, and God said to Moses, "When I see the blood, I will pass over you." I imagined there would be a prominent Jewish family in which the oldest daughter was named Sarah. She was a lovely girl; she was obedient to her parents; she attended to the teaching of the rabbis and lived an exemplary life. On the evening that the Lord had designated, she was studying at her books when she called to her father, "Daddy, did you put blood on the outside of the door? Did not God tell Moses that every man must do it, and that the blood must be on every door?" She was quite interested because she was the firstborn in the family. The father replied, "No, dear, I have not put out blood because God did not mean this to apply to nice people like us and to lovely children like you. You must always take God's Word for what it means and not for what it says. Go back to your lessons, my daughter; your father knows best."

She did return to her lessons, but about 11:00 she was so disturbed that again she called her father and said, "Daddy, did God say that all the bad people must do it or that everybody must do it? You know, Daddy, I am the oldest one of the children, and I do not want to die." Her father was irritated by this persistence of his daughter and said rather sharply, "Sarah, I told you that you must not take God too literally. You know very well He was not talking about you because our home is a good home. He was talking about that family down the street that live such wicked lives. Go to bed, dear, and quit worrying; your father knows best." The dear girl was too distressed to go to bed and could not sleep. She had heard that God had said to Moses that every house must be sheltered under the blood. She knew there was no blood on the door of the home where she lived. Just before 12:00 midnight, she called her father again and said, "Daddy, I am awfully afraid, for there is no blood on our door, and God told Moses that the blood must be on every house."

As the clock struck 12:00, the father heard a strange noise and, hurrying to the bedroom of his daughter, found that she was lying dead on the floor. God had kept His word. The father had interpreted it to suit his own feelings and fancy. If he had put the blood on the doorpost, as he had been instructed, it would have shown to the angel that he believed God. The absence of the blood proved he did not believe God. I then continued addressing the audience with the plea that each one of them believe God, trust the living Saviour, and get under the blood of Calvary.

The lady on the front seat continued to weep as I told the story and as I concluded the service. An appeal was made for those who would trust Christ to rise and say so. Many of the young people did rise and in a very intelligent manner told that for the first time they had seen the value of Jesus

Christ and His death for them at Calvary. After the confessions were made, I left the platform and went to the weeping teacher to ask her the reason for her grief. She told me quickly that she was quite sure she had never come under the blood. She decided she was a hypocrite, a professing Christian who had never believed God about the Lord Jesus. This stirred my heart, and so I knelt beside her and said, "I certainly shall tell the Lord Jesus how He has neglected you. It isn't fair that He should shed His blood for others and omit you." Having said this to her, I began to pray and said, "Lord Jesus, I cannot understand why You neglected this woman and did nothing for her while You were dying for others." She took hold of my shoulder and exclaimed, "Don't tell Jesus that; that isn't right, and it isn't so!" Of course, I wanted her to see that fact, and so I said again to the Saviour, "Do tell this friend why You did nothing for her at Calvary. You shed Your blood for others; You died for sinners; why did You not do something for this person?" My friend exclaimed quickly, "How foolish it is to talk that way! Of course, the Saviour did not neglect me. He was dying for me, and He blotted my sins out—His Bible says so. However could I doubt it!" The peace of God filled her heart, and the joy of the Lord changed her countenance from sadness to smiles. Christ Jesus had become real and precious to her.

They Got What They Wanted

At 11:00 Sunday morning, just as I was ready to conduct a service at a Bible camp, a gentleman and his wife approached me and asked for an audience at the close of the meeting. This I was glad to grant. This couple took their places near the platform and listened quite intently as the Word of God was expounded. They had their Bibles with them and turned to the passages as I quoted the various Scriptures.

The service closed at 12:00, and since dinner was not to be served until 12:30, there was time for us to converse together. We sat down on some benches out under the trees near the tabernacle. Immediately the conversation was opened by the husband, who said, "We drove one hundred twenty-five miles this morning to see you. We both are distressed in our spirits and have been for quite some time because we cannot find what we want." I saw that they were both deeply in earnest, and so, of course, my curiosity was aroused. I sought to ascertain the cause of the trouble.

I asked them to tell me the source of the distress and promised to help them if I could. The wife answered quickly and said, "We want to be righteous and sinless and pure. We belong to —————— church in J.C., and our teachers teach us that we should be sinless and have no evil thoughts, desires, or actions. We want to be so clean and pure that we can go to heaven when we die. We want to be as nearly perfect as possible, so we can be what Jesus wants us to be. We have been trying for years to get to the place where we felt that all of our sins were gone, and we would have no evil thoughts. We have prayed for this; we have read our Bibles to find the answer; we have cried out our hearts' desire to God many times. Somehow it always evades us, and we find ourselves back where we started. One thing we cannot understand, Dr. Wilson, is that the preachers who preach these things to us are not sinless themselves. I know this because the preachers who visit our church live in our home, and they are no different from us. They sin just as we do. Please tell us what God's answer is to this problem because we must have peace about it."

This battle that was going on in the hearts of these two is a rather common battle in the minds of those who, desiring to be right with God, do not know how to get that blessing. Since these two friends had their well-worn Bibles with them, and I saw that they wanted God's thoughts about their difficulties, I asked them to turn to Romans 5:17. They did so, and we read in that verse that some "receive abundance of grace and of the gift of righteousness." I asked them to notice also in verse 18 that the righteousness of the Lord Jesus is a gift for all men and brings justification with it. They had never seen this truth before and did not know that God's righteousness is obtained as a gift and not as a reward. I also called their attention to Romans 3:22, where we read that the righteousness of God "is by faith of Jesus Christ." That also was a new thought to them, for they had been led to believe that they could obtain righteousness by self-effort.

We were going over these points very slowly as they read the passages in their own Bibles, and I could see by their expressions that it was not altogether clear to them. I therefore had them turn to Romans 10:3. I said to them, "Perhaps you are seen in this verse as those who are ignorant of God's righteousness and are going about to establish your own righteousness. You have not succeeded very well. You have found that there is no peace in pursuing that path, and so today I want you to notice that God's righteousness is a gift to you the moment you trust Jesus Christ."

There seemed to be some ray of hope now in the hearts of these friends, and they were waiting for a clear explanation of this wonderful truth. I asked them to turn to Romans 4:6. We read verse 5 for the connection, and then I commented on the statement, "Blessed is the man unto whom God imputeth righteousness without works." They seemed to be puzzled by the expression and asked for an explanation. I sought to help them to understand the passage by using the illustration of the commoner who marries the king and immediately becomes the queen of the country. The position of the king as the head of the nation is imputed to the wife, and she is the queen only because she belongs to the king. I told them of the poor girl who was courted by a millionaire and married him. Immediately his credit standing and his social standing were imputed to the girl, who was so poor before they were married.

So it is with God the Father. His Son, the Lord Jesus, is rich in righteousness, holiness, grace, and purity. When we fall in love with Him, believe in Him, receive Him, and become His own bride, then God the Father imputes to us all the place, position, character, and standing of His Son, Christ Jesus. His righteousness becomes ours. His holiness and purity are given to us. These are gifts from God because we belong to His Son.

All the time I was explaining this to them, they were intently looking at the passage, Romans 4:5-6. I was praying to the Holy Spirit that He would enlighten their minds and reveal the value of Christ to their hearts. Suddenly the light of heaven shone upon them, and they both saw the truth of imputed righteousness for them. Rising quickly from their seats, they threw their arms about each other. The tears were coursing down their cheeks, and they could hardly speak. I heard them say, "I see it! I see it! God gives us righteousness because we trust His Son." They sat down again, still weeping, remained in silence for a few moments, and then said, "We never saw those passages in the Bible before. We belong to Jesus Christ, and God has made us righteous right now. Our prayers are answered, and our search is ended. Why didn't our preachers tell us this wonderful truth long ago?"

They rose to leave for the dinner table and then decided they would not stay for lunch. They were so filled with joy and peace that they decided to hurry back home and to tell their fellow church members the marvelous deliverance they had found and the precious, wonderful truth of the gift of righteousness.

I trust that many other hungry hearts reading this message will find the truth so often given in the Scriptures, "The Lord is our righteousness."

God Visited
the Circus

Upon one occasion, it so happened that in the mail placed upon my desk there was a letter from a radio friend in southern Kansas which told a story of unusual interest. She said that her sister held a prominent position in one of the large circuses touring the country. Her habit was to mail copies to this sister of my morning radio messages, and these had stirred her heart quite deeply. Several letters had passed back and forth between them about the subject of salvation and Christian living.

A recent letter which had been received by my radio friend from her sister contained a request. This particular circus was soon to play in Kansas City, and the request was that she might have an opportunity to see me for a personal conference concerning the need of her own soul. Of course my radio friend sent the request on to me at Kansas City, and I looked forward with pleasure and anticipation to this conference.

In due time, the circus came to the city to play for two days. On the second day, I went out about half-past one in the afternoon in search of this sister. Her husband was at the front door of the show and directed me to the place in the "big top" where I would find his wife.

"I am sure," he said, "you will receive a cordial welcome from her, for she has been looking forward to seeing you and told me to send you in as soon as you came."

Thanking him, I soon found my way to where the woman was working. As soon as she saw me, her whole countenance changed. A deep sadness and sorrow were evident. "I am so glad you have come," she said, extending her hand for a greeting. "My sister has been writing me of your messages, and I would like so much to talk with you about my own need."

"When may I have that privilege?" I asked.

"As soon as the grand entry begins, I will be free," she replied, "and I will meet you out at the front door. Will you wait for me there?"

Assenting to this, I went out to the front of the show, and there waited for perhaps thirty minutes or more until she came.

We went over to one side of the marquee, where we could be more or less quiet and where she could tell me of her soul's interest. It seemed that several of the radio messages about the meeting with God, the final judgment, God's wrath against sin, and the marks of a true Christian life had all been used by the Holy Spirit to reveal to her the need of a Saviour.

"Do you believe that the Lord Jesus came to save sinners, Mrs. O————?" I asked. "You know about Him of course. Did God really send Him to save you? What is your attitude toward Him?"

She immediately replied, "I do not know; I wish I did. I know there is a Saviour, but I do not know how He saves sinners. I want to know; I want Him to save me."

Taking my Bible out of my pocket, I read to her John 5:24: "Verily, verily, I say unto you, He that heareth my word, and believeth on him that sent me, hath everlasting life, and *shall not come into condemnation* [judgment]; but is passed from death unto life."

On one side of us, the sideshow banners, partly lowered, were flapping in the wind. Just behind them the band in the sideshow was beating out a medley of noises and a din that lacked much of making real harmony. Behind us was the menagerie, and over to the left was the "big-top" with the band playing for the various acts. What a place for a soul to be saved! The people were coming and going. A group of about thirty men were pulling and tightening the ropes of the tent. The candy-butchers were offering their products here and there, and those on the concession stands directly in front of us were crying out their wares. And yet God came into that scene in a wonderful way. In the midst of all the noises, the Prince of Peace was bringing peace.

The Scripture which we read together seemed to interest my friend greatly. She looked on the page in order to read it for herself. We re-read it together, slowly and carefully. I called her attention to each word, showing her that the Lord Jesus Himself was speaking; that He was inviting her to believe His Word and asking her to believe that God sent Him to save her; that He was promising her that the moment she would accept Him and give herself to Him, that He would immediately give her everlasting life, blot out every sin-stain, and make her a child of God.

As she listened intently to the message and followed the verse through again and again, she suddenly turned and asked, "If I trust in Jesus Christ today, will that save me from going to the judgment, as this verse seems to indicate? If so, why will I not go to the judgment? I do not understand."

What a pleasure it was to explain to her that the moment she trusted the Lord Jesus, He would immediately blot out the adverse record in heaven, would write her name in the book of life, and would cleanse her from every sin-stain. Since no sins would be left, there would be nothing to go to the judgment for. I explained that Christ took the punishment for her at Calvary. We read together Isaiah 53:5, in which it is written: "He was wounded for our transgressions, he was bruised for our iniquities; the chastisement of our peace was upon him; and with his stripes we are healed." Again we read in 1 Peter 3:18, "Christ also hath once suffered for sins, the just for the unjust, that he might bring us to God."

"That is quite clear to me now," she said. "I under-stand it and see how it is that He can save the one who trusts Him."

She then bowed her head quietly and said, "Lord Jesus Christ, I receive You just now, and I know that You take me. I thank You for doing so much for me on the Cross, and I will seek to live for You now that I have trusted You. Thank You, Lord Jesus."

As she looked up, I noticed that her cheeks were wet, but the peace of God could be seen in her countenance. She had found rest in trusting Jesus Christ. Have you found rest in Him? If not, trust Him today as she did.

A few days after this happy occasion, Mrs. O———— resigned from the circus, and with her husband she entered a small business enterprise in an eastern city, where she became affiliated with a local group of Christians.

The Wrong Address, But the Right Persons

The train had just entered the boundary limits of a great city when the porter aroused me from my deep sleep and informed me that we would soon be in the depot. There was no time for reading the Word, nor for a season of prayer, for the train had come to a stop by the time I was fully dressed, and all the passengers were leaving.

Because I intended spending only a day in that city, I checked my baggage at the station, took my sample case, and went at once to the office of my customer. At 4:00, after completing our business transactions together, I left him and started back to the station. Because I had been deprived of my morning period of meditation, this lack of spiritual food and preparation not only caused me to feel heavy of heart, but it also filled my soul with disappointment as I walked down the street.

A large hotel was located on that street. Entering, I went up to the mezzanine floor where I sought to be alone with the Lord. I confessed to Him my failure that day, my neglect of prayer, and also my omission to read the Scriptures. I then asked Him whether in His infinite grace He would not find some way to give a message through my lips to some troubled heart in that strange city. Having waited on the Lord a while, I felt convinced that He would find some work to do through me that evening.

About 5:30, while sitting in the coffee shop, the Lord reminded me that there abode in that city the son of a friend of mine who lived out West. I knew that this son was not saved and at once accepted it as from the Lord that I should visit this young man and give him the gospel. Obtaining a telephone book, I soon found his address and decided to call at his home. Arriving there, I found a duplex building with his name on a plate by the door leading upstairs. I rang the bell which opened the door, permitting me to enter the hall. At the top of the stairs stood a young woman who inquired what I wanted. I was not surprised to see a young woman, for I had been told that my young friend had recently been married.

"Is this where Charlie Johnson lives?" I asked. "I am a friend of his and came to visit him."

"Yes, come right up," she invited, very courteously.

As I reached the top of the stairs, she escorted me into a very attractive living room, nicely furnished but dimly lit. On the opposite side of the room stood a lady and a gentleman, whom she introduced to me as the sister and brother-in-law of Mr. Johnson. Taking my overcoat and hat, they invited me to be seated, whereupon I inquired whether or not Charlie was at home.

My heart was impressed with the opportunity presented of giving the gospel, and I was much in prayer that the Holy Spirit would give the right words and would guide in the conversation. In reply to my inquiry, Mrs. Johnson said: "I am sorry, but Charlie is not home; he is working nights now."

"How splendid that is," I said. "His business must have increased greatly since he has found it necessary to put on both a day and a night shift."

She looked quite surprised upon hearing this and said, "Charlie is not in business; he is an engineer and just now is working on a night shift at the city waterworks."

"Is not his father a merchant in Loganville?" I asked.

"Why no," she said, "his father is a carpenter and lives in Jackson. I married him there."

A look of astonishment came over all our faces, for it was quite evident that I was in the wrong house. "I cannot understand this," I said, "for Charlie's father told me that he was engaged in manufacturing small motors for washing machines and that he was doing quite well at the business. It is evident that I have secured the wrong address of my friend, and I shall leave. I trust you will pardon me for intruding, and I am sorry if your evening's visit has been interrupted by my coming."

Mrs. Johnson smiled, while all three of them arose to tell me good-bye. "I believe I know what your trouble is, Doctor," she said. "There is another Charlie Johnson who lives at this same number and on this same street, but he lives on the east side of town; we are on the west side. His home is just forty blocks straight east of us on this very street. I know that his father lives in Loganville, for we get his mail frequently, and I have noticed the postmark on the envelope."

This peculiar coincidence caused my heart to cry out to God, for I felt that this visit was planned by the Lord. Many thoughts were going through my mind while I put on the overcoat. Approaching the center of the room to bid good-bye to the sister and her husband, I observed, lying on the center table, a well-worn Bible with dog-eared corners. I knew that dog-ears on books could not be purchased at the bookstore. These come only by long and frequent usage. Picking up the Bible, carefully and prayerfully I inquired, "Do you read this book, Mrs. Johnson, and do you love it?" At once all three of them became deeply interested. They looked at each other with astonishment and then at me, as though their minds were stirred to ask some important question. "Yes," she answered quickly and firmly. "We love that Book in this home."

"Have you found out from its pages how you may be saved and know it?" I inquired.

By this time the hearts of these friends were so stirred that they could not restrain the tears. They looked at each other in such a peculiar way that I sensed immediately that some strange thing was transpiring with which I was not familiar. After she regained control of her feelings, Mrs.

Johnson asked, "Do you understand that Bible? Can you tell us how we may be saved?"

"Yes, indeed, that is my principal business in life," I assured her. "I would be so glad if I could help you with it."

She urged me to remove my overcoat again and to be seated. We had drawn up our chairs near the table and were comfortably seated when Mrs. Johnson said, "Dr. Wilson, when you rang the doorbell, we three were on our knees praying that God would send someone to show us the way of salvation. We have been meeting here every Friday night to pray for help. All summer long we have gone to services here and there and have heard some wonderful messages. Somehow none of these sermons have helped us. What we want to know is how to get rid of our sins and to obtain eternal life. We know that Jesus does it, but how does He do it? Can you answer this question?"

It was not difficult to see that the blessed Lord of the harvest had answered my prayer and led me to the very place where the Lord Jesus was working and wanted to enter in. Each one obtained a Bible, while I took mine from my pocket, and we all turned to Luke 19:10. There we found the statement of the Lord Jesus, saying, "The Son of man is come to seek and to save that which was lost."

"It is you three that He came to save," I continued. "Your heart should be very glad indeed to know that God saw your need and provided for you a Saviour who is both able and willing to save. Will you let Him save you tonight?"

Their faces now were aglow with anticipation. They were drinking in every word and reading the message for themselves out of their own Bibles. Mrs. Johnson then asked, "But how does He save anyone, Doctor? That is exactly what we want to know."

Turning to 1 Peter 3:18, we read aloud, "Christ also hath once suffered for sins, the just for the unjust, that he might bring us to God." "By suffering for you," I explained to them, "He took the punishment for your sin; He took the whipping you should have had. God made Him suffer for your sins that you might trust Him with the saving of your soul and enjoy God's favor and forgiveness."

We then turned to 1 Peter 2:24 and read, "Who his own self bare our sins in his own body on the tree." "He bore them for you three friends," I said. "It was your own sins which God laid upon Him and took from you. God now invites you to accept the Lord Jesus as His gift to you. He is at God's right hand, able to save, and He will save you now, if you will trust Him with your soul."

Hesitating here in the conversation, I perceived that these three friends, while observing each other, were apparently meditating as though permitting the Word of God to bring light to their hearts. Presently Mrs. Johnson arose and said, slowly and deliberately, "We want to take Christ and are ready to accept Him right now; we have just been waiting through these long months for someone to tell us how we could come to Him and how He would save us."

"Let us kneel together then," I suggested, "and tell Him so." We knelt around the table, and each one of them spoke personally to Christ, thanking Him for dying for them and bearing their sins away. They spoke to God and thanked Him for sending Jesus to save them from their sins. What a precious sight it was that night to see these three turn to Christ and find in Him all that their hungry souls longed for!

After we arose, I told them the interesting story of my experience that day; how I had looked to the Spirit of God to plan the evening for His glory; how I had given to Him again my lips and my feet that He might through the use of them find some troubled hearts. We thanked the Lord together for the wrong address where I found the right persons ready to receive the redeeming grace of God.

What a joy it is to the Christian worker when the discovery is made that the Spirit is ready and willing to direct us to that home or that heart where He is working and where He wants us to deliver His message. Let us learn to expect and rely upon His guidance in our daily lives.

Saved Above the Clouds

The Lord Jesus came "to seek and to save that which was lost." The lost one might be in a submarine at the bottom of the sea, or it might be a nurse in a busy ward, or a railroad engineer beside his engine, or a policeman on the beat. The case I shall relate to you here is that of a hostess serving on a plane eastbound from Kansas City. She was a young lady of about twenty-five years, very pleasant in her attitude toward the passengers, and quite accommodating to the mothers with babies. As soon as we were at the altitude where we were to fly, she checked in the passengers. As she passed through the plane, writing down the names of the passengers, she came to me and saw that I had my Bible open and was preparing to read. She did not remark about it but continued through the plane until her records were finished.

I had a window seat, and the aisle seat was vacant. After a while Miss W———— came and sat down beside me and made the remark, "What strange book is that you are reading?" I was quite surprised at the statement and the question, for I did not suppose there was anyone in our great country who did not recognize a Bible at once on seeing it. I replied that this was the Bible, sometimes called the Scriptures and usually called the Word of God. I said to her, "Do you not have a Bible, Miss W————?" She answered, "No, I have never had one. I have been raised like a heathen. My mother belonged to one church, and my father to another church, and neither one wanted me to go to the church of the other. Neither one of them had a Bible, and so I have just been in the dark all the time about that Book. I had heard about it and thought that perhaps some day my curiosity would be satisfied, and I would learn something about it. When I saw you with that strange Book, I thought perhaps you could help me."

I replied that I was very happy indeed to tell her about the contents of the Book. I said, "This Book is mostly about you and the Lord Jesus." This was quite a surprise to her, and her interest deepened. She answered me by saying, "Tell me what the Book says about me." I did so by reading to her Romans 3:10-18. I told her that this passage was God's description of her. It is not what your friends think about you, nor even your enemies. It is not what you think about yourself or your neighbors. God is revealing in this passage what He thinks about you, as He looks down from heaven and sees your life, your words, your character, and your deeds. She listened most intently as I explained these verses to her and called her attention to the universal character of the passage. It says we are *all* under sin, none righteous, none that understands, none that seeks after God, all gone out of the way, none that doeth good, and the way of peace have they not known.

She turned to me and with deep earnestness said, "How could they know all about me and describe me so fully? For those verses certainly tell what I am." It was my turn to be surprised, for I cannot remember when any moral, upright, lovely person, as she seemed to be, immediately accepted God's diagnosis of the case. My answer was, "The Holy Spirit told Paul what to write about you because He knows all about you, for He is on earth listening to every word and understanding all the thoughts." For a few moments she was a bit stunned. The thought of her condition being written down so clearly in the Scriptures amazed her. Then she said to me, "What does the Bible say about Jesus?" This invitation indicated to me that the Holy Spirit was dealing

with this young lady in a very definite way. I read to her
Matthew 1:21: "Thou shalt call His name Jesus: for He shall
save His people from their sins." I also read to her that
beautiful, well-known verse, John 3:16, and explained to her
that God had sent the Lord Jesus, His own Son, to put away
her sins by His precious blood so that she would never perish
and to give her eternal life so she could live with God.

She seemed to understand readily that she needed to
take the gift of Jesus Christ, whom God had given to her.
In order to help her to see this more fully, I read John 1:12:
"But as many as received Him, to them gave He power to
become the sons of God." I added to that 1 John 5:12: "He
that hath the Son hath life." She meditated a few minutes
on this wonderful truth, then bowed her head and said, "Lord
Jesus, I see from the Bible that God sent You to me to
save me. I want You to do it right now. I have wanted
to be a Christian, but never knew how and never knew about
Your Book. Now I am trusting You, and I thank You that
You have blotted out my sins."

She was called away at this point to take care of a
passenger that was in need, and very shortly we arrived at
the airport in Chicago and landed. I waited behind and let
the other passengers get off the plane so that I could be
the last one to speak to Miss W————. I shook hands
with her at the door and said, "Miss W————, what is
the Lord Jesus to you?" She replied with happy animation,
"Dr. Wilson, He is my Saviour. He put away my sins. God
gave Him to me, and I belong to Him. I surely am going
to tell my friends all about it."

And so we parted, having had a meeting with the
Saviour through the sweet influence and guidance of the Holy
Spirit up above the clouds. It can happen anywhere. Let
each one of us be sure we have a tryst with Christ wherever
we may be.

No Chair in the Temple

My chum had moved to California to enter the field of agriculture, particularly with the thought of studying more fully methods of grafting, transplanting, and other experimental work with plant life. He purchased several acres in the vicinity of Los Angeles and began to plant various kinds of bushes, trees, vines, etc., on which he expected to spend his efforts in making the products of these plants larger, sweeter, and better.

At this time I had an injury to my back, and, after having the back operated on to relieve the difficulty, I decided to go to California for a rest and to seek to recover sufficiently so that I could remove the plaster cast which I was wearing. I wrote my friend George that I was coming, and he invited me to be his guest in his home. I had known his wife since she was a little girl, and she joined heartily in the invitation. My stay lasted seven weeks and was most enjoyable and profitable, for I was able to remove the cast and found myself quite well again. My chum would receive no remuneration from me for all his kindness and expense, so I looked around the house to see if there was a need of any particular bit of furniture that I might supply. I noticed that they did not have sufficient bookcase room for all their books. Books were lying on the table, on the floor, and on shelves in the closet.

This I thought would be something I could supply to fill a real need in that home. I therefore went up to the business district of the little city and found an attractive furniture store in which there was quite a display of chairs. I entered the store and was looking around the room to see if I could find any sectional bookcases, but I saw none. As I was observing the many chairs, an elderly lady approached me and asked if she might be of some use in helping me to find what I wanted. I told her that I was seeking some sectional bookcases but failed to see any. She replied that they had quite a good stock of these in various colors, but that they were in the rear of the store, and two clerks were working in that department now with some customers. She assured me that she would take me to them and would try to find for me just the kind I wanted.

Just when she had promised me her help, I mentioned that she seemed to have a very unusual line of beautiful chairs. And then I added, "Do you know that the most beautiful building in all the world, and the most expensive building ever built, did not contain a chair, nor a seat of any kind?" She was astonished at this statement and asked me to sit down and tell her more about it. She herself sat down and waited for my explanation. I said to her, "Solomon built a temple, which was covered all over on the inside with matched cedar, and the cedar was covered with thick plates of gold. Even the floor was covered with these golden plates. The five pieces of furniture that were in the building were made of pure gold; or, if they were made of wood, then that was covered with thick, pure gold. In addition to this, there were sockets on the walls of this beautiful, golden room, and magnificent gems of many kinds, the finest in the world, were set in these golden sockets so that the light from the candlesticks would cause them to give forth beautiful, radiating, colored beams of light. But in all of this, there was no chair or bench."

This lady expressed her astonishment as she said, "I have been in the church for many years; I have been a leader in that church and attended services constantly, but I never heard anything like this before. Is that building described in the Bible?" I assured her that it was and that she would find the record in 2 Chronicles 2-5. Now her curiosity was so aroused that she asked me why there was no chair in this beautiful building. I wanted her to ask that question because that was the key to the truth I intended to convey to her. I answered her question by saying, "The priests in the temple never finished their work. The people kept sinning and bringing their offerings, and the priests found it necessary to be constantly serving, constantly offering sacrifices, and constantly meeting the spiritual needs of those who came with their sheep, their turtledoves, or their bullocks. Because of this constant need, the priests must be constantly serving, and therefore there were no chairs or places of rest in this magnificent building. The contrast to this is found in Hebrews 1:3, which reads, 'When he had by himself purged our sins, sat down on the right hand of the Majesty on high.' His work was finished for the sinner. No more sacrifice was necessary. All the sins of the believer were blotted out. There was no need for another sacrifice, for 'by one offering he hath perfected forever them that are sanctified.' "

Again my friend looked at me in complete astonishment and repeated that in all her Christian life she had not known this truth, nor did she know it was contained in the Bible. There was no antagonism in the spirit of this friend, but only a feeling of disappointment that she had never been told nor taught this wonderful truth from the Scriptures. Her mind was open, and her spirit receptive. I waited for her to reply, and she said, "I certainly do appreciate this revelation of God's way of salvation. Of course, the priest could not sit down if his work was not finished. We do the same thing in this store. My clerks do not sit down if there are customers to be served." This revealed to me that my friend with whom I was conversing was evidently the owner of this lovely store, and I asked her if she was. She replied that she was the sole owner, for her husband had died and left this business to her. Then she added, "I am glad the Lord Jesus finished the work for me so that I can sit down and enjoy the wonderful blessing of being saved by Him. If I had known this years ago, it would have saved me many hours of worrying and of distress. Deep in my heart I knew that I was not living as I should, so I worked harder at my religion and yet had no peace or relief. Thank you so much for telling me this wonderful message. I will never forget it. When I look at these chairs from now on, I will remember that when He had purged my sins, He sat down because the work was done. I will love Him now in a new way because of what He means to me."

Now that the great work of salvation was finished, she led me back into another department where I saw quite a variety of sectional bookcases. I selected five of these in the color that I thought would match the sitting room of my friend. I paid for them and instructed the owner of the store to make delivery to the house of my friend, which was done the next day. So two transactions were finished: my new friend took the Saviour, and my host took the bookcases. It was the end of a perfect day.

The Lawyer and His Judge

The subject of the radio message on a certain morning was "The Five Judgments of God." I took up briefly the Judgment of the Great White Throne, the Judgment Seat of Christ, the Judgment of Calvary, the Judgment of the Sheep and Goats, and the Judgment of One's Own Self. A very prominent lawyer of the city was listening in his home as the message was given, and because it pertained to those things with which he was familiar in his daily occupation, he gave very close attention to the message of the speaker.

Before leaving the radio room I received a telephone call from this attorney requesting me to take lunch at the noon hour with him as his guest. This invitation was gladly accepted, and arrangements were made to meet in the Savoy Lunch Room at 12:15.

I was not personally acquainted with this attorney, but I knew that he was quite active in one of the larger churches of the city and was known as an active and successful builder of a large Bible class of men. This class bore the name of this man, so it was known as the "Harris Men's Bible Class." There were about five hundred men enrolled, and they met each Sunday morning to be enthused and stirred by the leadership of this lawyer. Mr. Harris did not teach the class but engaged other men whom he thought were better qualified.

All during the morning I pondered over this engagement and wondered why a man of such prominence and ability should wish to have a conference with me. He was a very prominent person in legal circles and held a political position of much power. I had often wondered about his class, as to whether Christ was known there and whether the members heard the gospel. The daily newspapers often carried stories concerning the class and their activities among the poor and the crippled and in civic improvement enterprises. The class gave liberally to needy families at Christmas time and in the summer season sponsored a camp for boys and another for girls.

I wondered whether my new friend would like counsel and advice concerning this social service work, or whether he might wish to talk with me about the interests of some friend who perhaps was in difficulty with the law. Never having had personal contact with Mr. Harris, I was quite in the dark concerning the desire for this meeting.

At 12:15 I met Mr. Harris at the Savoy Lunch Room as appointed. He knew me at once and made himself known to me, for he had been in some of my services without identifying himself. We were soon seated together at a table for two in this beautiful, colonial restaurant and proceeded to order the meal. We conversed together about various local and national matters of public interest while waiting for the meal to be served. After the waitress had placed the food before us and we had begun to partake of it, I said to my friend, "Mr. Harris, what was on your mind when you invited me to have this lunch with you? Do you have some problem that I may confer with you about? Do you have any burden on your heart that I might share with you? Do feel quite free to tell me anything you wish, for I shall regard our conversation as confidential."

This invitation seemed to relieve the heart of Mr. Harris so that he felt free to tell me the real cause for our conference. He did not reply immediately but seemed a bit confused as to just how and where to begin his conversation. I waited quietly for him to answer. "Do you know the work in which I am engaged?" he asked.

I replied, "Not exactly, Mr. Harris. I do know your official position in the city, and I have read in the paper of your activities at the Barnard Church where you have built up such a large Bible class. I have no direct information about you or your faith, and I only know what I have read. I should like very much to have you tell me something about yourself, if it fits in with your desire at the present time."

Mr. Harris was not eating his meal as though he enjoyed it. He seemed to be only tasting the various foods without much interest or appetite. His mind was evidently on things that were more important, and his interests were deeper than the satisfying of his physical hunger. He began his story quietly and earnestly. "For many years I have been practicing law in this city, as you perhaps know. My ability has been recognized, and for that reason I have received a vote of confidence from the public which placed me in my present excellent position. During this time I have felt the desire for religion in my life. Being naturally a leader of men, I started this Bible class at the Barnard Church with the thought of increasing my own religious conceptions and also of bringing into Christianity a lot of men who would be more attracted by businessmen than they would by a preacher. I found some good singers among the men that came and some good, enthusiastic workers. We have put on 'PEP' meetings and 'PEP' songs to work up the enthusiasm. We appointed team captains to increase the attendance. We offered prizes for the largest attendance by sections, and also individual rewards for those who would bring the largest number of men at one meeting or during the course of the month.

"The scheme has worked splendidly as you know. We have one of the largest classes in the Valley, and the fellows certainly do take an interest in every opportunity for doing good that is presented to them."

Mr. Harris had told the truth about this group of men. They were enthusiastic about the class and about their various administrations of help where opportunity offered. They had a name in the city of being very liberal and very thorough in their work. Of course, Mr. Harris received the credit for managing such a large and efficient group and was accorded quite a little recognition by the churches of the community as well as by the city officials.

While Mr. Harris was giving me this information, I was asking the Holy Spirit to cause him to open his heart to me fully. I was also asking for wisdom in making a reply. I could see that something was wrong with Jack (for that was his name). I knew that he had not told me all the story. His conversation had thus far sounded as sort of a preamble to the real story of his heart. As he paused a little in recounting this much of his life, I said to him, "Tell me, Mr. Harris, whether all of this activity has satisfied the hunger of your heart. Do you feel that what you have done and what you are doing is enough to meet your need and to satisfy the demand of your God? How do you feel about it, Mr. Harris?"

Evidently this inquiry was exactly what he had wanted to hear. It seemed to relieve the restraint that was in his mind and to remove any doubt as to my interest in his welfare. We should always seek to make it easy for people to unburden their hearts to us; otherwise, they will hold back the real secret and will hide from us the matter that should be exposed.

The meal was becoming cold while we conversed and studied each other. I was seeking to diagnose the case of my patient, and he was examining me to see whether he could confide in me and unburden his soul to me. Neither of us cared much for the food. The Spirit of God was hovering over us. The solemnity of eternity had made itself felt. We drew near to the vital point of the conversation with a sense of the presence of God.

He answered me shortly by saying, "Doctor, I listened to your message on the radio this morning concerning the Judgments, and it stirred me deeply. I have been practicing law long enough to know that a guilty man cannot be acquitted before the judge and the jury have all the facts plainly placed before them. Sometimes the lawyer for the defense is clever and is able to turn the attention of the jury from the facts to his own deductions and conclusions, but this scheme will never work in God's court, and I know it. I have seen defense lawyers, by clever manipulation, prevent the introduction into the trial of evidence that is of very great importance. I know that this can never be done in the court of heaven, where Christ has charge of the proceedings. He is a righteous Judge."

The logic of this honest heart and splendid legal mind appealed to me very much. I saw at once that I was not dealing with one who thought carelessly or decided foolishly. There was an earnestness here that appealed to my heart. I looked to the Spirit of God again with joy because of this wonderful opportunity to help a darkened heart. Mr. Harris was a younger man by some years than I, so I felt free to ask his permission to call him by his given name. He gladly assented.

"Jack," I said, "there will never be any such perversion of justice in God's court. You are right in what you said. I am glad that you recognize that God will deal with us in righteousness. Tell me more about your thoughts in this matter."

He was eager to continue and replied, "As you gave the message this morning on the Judgment of the Great White Throne, it made me very uneasy. I asked myself the question 'How will I ever get through that Judgment?' My life has had lots of sin in it, and He has the evidence against me. There is no use my pleading extenuating circumstances. There is no use my pleading an alibi. God has the evidence against me, and I cannot deny it. I tell you, Dr. Wilson, it has troubled me tremendously all morning. I have been able to save some guilty men from punishment in my legal practice, but it will never work in heaven."

My heart was rejoicing in the conclusions which Jack had reached. I could see plainly that the Lord had been dealing with this heart and was leading him straight to the Saviour. I saw that the Holy Spirit had already convicted him and that his desire now was to find a way out.

"What are you going to do about it, Jack?" I inquired.

"I do not know, Dr. Wilson," he answered. "That is the reason I sent for you. I want you to tell me. I cannot and must not go on without knowing the remedy."

This answer filled my heart with a greater joy, and taking my Bible I opened it to John 5:24 and gave it to him to read. He did read it slowly and carefully. I asked him to read the verse several times, and he did so. "I do not understand it." he said. "What does it mean to believe? I have always believed that the Bible was true. I have never questioned it or doubted it."

The problem he presented was one that is common among men. Everywhere we find those who are unsaved affirming that they agree with all that is in the Bible and have no doubts concerning its veracity.

"Jack," I said, "to believe the facts is good, but the blessing comes when you appropriate them. You believe that this food is wholesome, but it will not help you until you partake of it. You believe that medicine is potent and pure, but it will not relieve you until you take it. You believe that the streetcar will take you downtown, but you must get on it in order to receive the benefit. So it is in this case. The Lord Jesus came to save you. God sent Him to do it, but you must receive Him and turn your case over to Him individually. You handle the cases of only those clients who commit themselves to your care; so Christ saves only those who turn themselves, with all their sins, over to Him."

This explanation brought a new light and a new hope to Jack's heart. He could see at once the analogy between himself with his client and the Lord Jesus with the sinner.

"Do you not see, Jack, that the Lord Jesus can blot out your sins, put away your guilt, and win your case at the Judgment only when you have trusted Him to do it? He is there at God's right hand, a living Man on the throne, in His own body of flesh and bones, ready and willing and able to take every case that is committed to His trust and handle that case successfully before the Supreme Bench. If you will trust Him just now, He will blot out the sin-stains; He will remove your guilt; He will make you His child."

I turned to John 3:16 and let him read the story of God's gift to him. Then we read in Isaiah 44:22: "I have blotted out, as a thick cloud, thy transgressions, and, as a cloud, thy sins: return unto Me; for I have redeemed thee." These passages were used of the Lord to reveal to Jack the ability and sufficiency of the Lord Jesus Christ to blot out the records that were against his soul.

He looked at me most earnestly, his face flushed and as he trembled with emotion, said, "I see those facts as I have never seen them before. I accept Jesus Christ, and I believe that He accepts me."

We bowed our heads in thanksgiving, and while he told the Saviour that he trusted Him, I praised the Holy Spirit for revealing the Lord Jesus to this needy lawyer.

As we separated at the close of the meal, Jack went back to his office with a load off his heart, and I went back to my work happy to have been with Christ when He saved a human soul.

How blessed it is to watch the Lord deal with men, revealing their need and then supplying a sufficient remedy. The remedy is always found in the Person of the living Lord. Let us remember that it is not the work of Christ that saves, but the Person of Christ. We trust the Lord Jesus Himself personally, and He applies His blessed and sufficient work to our souls. He makes the precious blood avail to the cleansing of our sins as we trust ourselves to Him. "He that hath the Son hath life" (1 John 5:12).

Lillian Was Miserable on the Stage

On one of the great theater circuits, there appeared a bright, happy, dark-haired girl, who by her dancing and singing had won the hearts of many. She seemed never to have a care. She was attractive in appearance, delightful in conversation, and radiated happiness to those whom she met. This was Lillian in the public eye and on the stage.

In the dressing room and in the hotel Lillian was quite a different girl. There she frequently wiped the tears from her eyes; deep sighs would come from her heart. Sometimes after the performance she would retire to her room, throw herself across the bed, and sob out her sorrow of heart.

Lillian's husband was afflicted with tuberculosis. He had been on the stage with her at various times, and as a team they were in much demand. Now Willard was lying on his back, wasting away with that dreaded white plague, while Lillian was seeking to pay the bills by appearing in an individual sketch. It seemed most convenient for Willard to remain in Kansas City for medical treatment, for Lillian was frequently in and out of this center as she filled her engagements. As her husband continued to grow worse, the darkness in Lillian's heart became a greater burden, until she felt that she could hardly continue on the stage in her hypocrisy.

One day her distress was so great that at the close of her afternoon performance she asked the stagehands if there was any downtown church where she might go to find relief from the distress of her heart. They replied that they did not know of such a church, for they were not churchgoing men. One of them volunteered the information that there was a factory down on Seventh Street where there were a lot of religious people who gave away tracts and Bibles. Perhaps she could get some help there. She immediately accepted the suggestion and found her way down to our plant.

From my desk in the private office, I observed a lady entering the salesroom, weeping as she came. I went out at once and said to her, "May I serve you in some way, my friend? I notice that you are weeping over some sorrow, and it would be a pleasure indeed if we might help you to bear it."

"I heard up at the theater from one of the stagehands that you people had Bibles and gospel tracts and probably would help me. Have you the time to listen to my story?"

"Yes, indeed," I replied, "it will be a pleasure to do so."

We retired to a private room in which conference meetings were often held and where prayer to God was made daily. Here, when we were seated, she told me the story of blighted hopes, thwarted ambitions, and the dying husband.

Matthew 11:28 was brought to my mind at once by the blessed Spirit of God as the passage which this young woman needed. I was delighted to see how the Holy Spirit had been working in her heart through the past years, on and off the stage. How blessed it is that He will work anywhere and will touch lives in every situation! He had given Lillian to see the utter emptiness of all that this world offers in the way of pleasure and popularity. Her husband was out of the race. Her own heart was broken. Her future was filled with darkness.

"Let me read you this verse, Lillian," I said, " 'Come unto me, all ye that labor and are heavy laden, and I will give you rest.' This is what your heart desires. This is what Christ is waiting to give you. He wants you to come directly to Him for His pardoning grace and His saving blood. 'Christ

Jesus came into the world to save sinners' is what we read in 1 Timothy 1:15. He came to save you. In saving you, He will give you rest. Would you not like Him to take away your sins and relieve your heart of your burden?"

"Yes," she replied. "My heart is just overburdened. It seems I can carry on no longer. I am at my wit's end and do not know which way to turn. I am not getting very much for my work on this circuit, and the illness of Willard takes it all as fast as I can get it. It is getting harder and harder for me to dance and sing with a smile on my face."

"Will you not read this verse again, Lillian," I inquired, and at the same time handed her my Bible opened at Matthew 11:28. She made no reply but read the verse. Over and over again she read it. The words entranced her. The call seemed to attract her. I could see that the person of Christ and the rest which He was offering to her troubled heart were enticing her to His side. Quietly she bowed her head in her hands and meditated on the passage. I remained quiet also, waiting to see what the Spirit of God would do to her heart. While waiting, I asked the Holy Spirit to reveal the Lord Jesus to Lillian's heart and to lift the load from her shoulders. I felt that He would not begin a good work in her and not finish it. While I was still praying, she spoke from her burdened heart and said, "I will come to the Lord Jesus Christ today; I want His rest; I need His peace; I need Him. How glad I am that He has invited me to come. I will lay the burden at His feet and will trust Him with my soul."

"Lillian, is Christ Jesus your own Saviour now?" I asked. "Have you really taken Him? Do you believe that He died to save you and is living now to forgive you? If you do, let us kneel together while you tell Him so. He is in heaven and can hear every word you say. Would you like to tell Him what you think of Him?"

She seemed eager to do so, as she replied, "Yes, if you will tell me how."

I answered, "We will kneel together, and I will tell Him that I am bringing you to Him by faith for His pardon and forgiveness; then you will tell Him that you are coming to trust Him. He is the living Saviour on His throne in heaven and will hear all that you say to Him."

We were soon on our knees in prayer. I told the Lord Jesus how glad I was to bring this lost sinner to Him for His salvation and redemption. Having finished, I said, "Now Lillian, you tell the Saviour what you think of Him."

She did so, and said, "Jesus, I come to You to be saved. I know You came to save sinners, and I want You to save me. You said that if I would come to You, You would give me rest. I believe You will, and so I do come to trust myself to You. Won't you bless Willard also? He doesn't know You, and he is dying. Do save my husband. Do help me to tell him about You in such a way that he will believe." Her weeping closed the prayer, and we arose from our knees to rejoice in the wonderful peace of God.

Let us ever be looking for troubled souls among those who are in the amusement world. Their hearts are heavy. They are not always in private what they are in public. Let us always be on the alert to find those who want help from heaven.

"Will I See My Little Girl Again?"

The story that I shall tell you just now is a most interesting one, but a rather unhappy one in that, in this instance, I failed to win my friend to the Lord Jesus Christ. The story is recorded because of its unusual character and in order to reveal the hopelessness of that heart that has no Christ, no Redeemer.

A gentleman from New York City, who was a Jew, frequently called at my office to sell trimmings for flags and banners. He offered gold and silver lace, fringes, spangles, and gold and silver fancy ornaments of various designs to be used in the manufacture of parade banners and regalia of lodges, Sunday schools, and other such groups. I had purchased from this firm for some years and was well acquainted with this salesman. We will call our friend Mr. Jacobs. He was a very hairy man, with thick, heavy eyebrows and a beard that covered much of his face.

One beautiful spring morning Mr. Jacobs came to my office making his semiannual call to see that our stock was complete on the merchandise which he sold. He spread out his samples on my table and named the new prices for the new year. I called the foreman of our banner department to the office and asked him to bring his stock sheet with him, which he did. We checked the requirements of the depleted stock, and I gave Mr. Jacobs an order for the materials which we anticipated we would need for the spring trade. Having finished this part of our engagement, my friend replaced the samples in his satchel and thanked me cordially for the order. Just at this point the Spirit suggested to me that I should speak to my friend about his soul. This story will relate what followed in this unusual conversation.

I began my inquiry by saying, "Mr. Jacobs, you have a good firm, you sell excellent merchandise, and the service that you render me is all that I could desire. I appreciate this very much. Because of our friendship and happy business relationship, I wonder if you would permit me to ask you a personal question?"

Mr. Jacobs pulled a chair up close to my desk, replaced his satchel on the floor, removed his hat, and said with much interest, "Certainly, Dr. Wilson. What would you like to ask me?"

I had not expected such a prompt and sympathetic reply, but, of course, was delighted that he should answer as he did. "I would like to ask you, Mr. Jacobs, whether you have a happy heart? You are always pleasant, and, on the surface, seem to have no cares or problems, and I have been wondering whether you do have any burdens or problems such as the rest of us experience."

Such a transformation came over the face of this man as I do not usually see. It seemed as though a blow had been struck that shocked and almost stunned him. For a moment he trembled and shook, and then he regained his composure. He did not immediately reply but turned his chair slightly away from me and turned his face still farther away, as he fought to prevent the exhibition of his emotions. I was quite surprised myself to see the unusual effect of my simple question. It is often the case that a smiling face hides a burdened heart. We cannot tell by appearances what is really going on beneath the surface. May the Holy Spirit give us wisdom and ability to discern the true condition of those whom we meet.

The grief of Mr. Jacobs became more apparent in a few moments. He leaned over on the desk, burying his face on his arm and sobbing greatly. I perceived that there was a hidden sorrow there which perhaps he would unveil to me if I should show a sympathetic attitude. This I was glad to do, and I said to him, "Mr. Jacobs, I see that you do have an unusual sorrow. Your grief touches my heart. Would you care to unburden yourself to me enough to permit me to sympathize with you and to share this load? I would be glad to do so, if permitted." This assurance to him of my sympathy seemed a great relief, and after regaining his composure he related to me, with some difficulty, the tragic story of the loss of his little Elizabeth.

It seems that this Jewish friend had fallen in love with a girl of the Catholic faith, Gertrude by name. They were married by a justice of the peace and shortly thereafter were excommunicated by their co-religionists. Mr. Jacobs was excommunicated because he had married a Catholic. Gertrude was dismissed from the Church because she had married a Jew. Both of them were without a spiritual home and without the support of their various ministers. After some time a precious baby girl came into this home and brought new sunshine and fresh, sweet joy to the hearts of these two who had been grieving because they were ostracized by both groups. Neither one of them cared to go to a Protestant service, and, therefore, they had mingled and mixed with the world of careless, godless friends.

Little Elizabeth knew nothing of God, for she was not permitted to hear the precious gospel. As she grew old enough to see and understand the things of life, they began taking her to shows, concerts, and places of pleasure during the evenings of the week and on Sunday. The little girl grew in these surroundings with no Christian influence. She had no knowledge of God, nor of Christ, nor of the Bible. Her whole outlook was that of this world, with no thought of the world to come.

How many children there are who are thus hindered and handicapped by their parents! How sad it is to think that these dear ones, so precious to their parents, are being raised to be lost forever as they grow to maturity! What a tragic day it will be when such parents face the Judge of all the earth and show cause why they should not receive an extra punishment for having thus robbed their children of the opportunity of becoming Christians!

But to return to my story, Mr. Jacobs began to tell me in the midst of his tears of the terrible tragedy that came into his life. His story in brief was this: One day as little Elizabeth, about eight years of age now, went to school, she got her feet wet in the rain and sat through school hours in the cold, wet clothing, which resulted in severe pneumonia. A very excellent physician was called in and began at once to prescribe the treatment for the sick little body. For several days it seemed as though the medicine would relieve the trouble, and the little one would recover. Of course, the father could not pray, and neither could the mother. They had not been taught to pray. They must just leave the case to the skill and care of the physician, for they were strangers to the Great Physician on the Throne.

At the close of the first week the doctor saw that he was losing ground and that this little life was in danger. Of course, there was great agony in the hearts of the parents, and they sought the help of a consulting physician. This learned gentleman, who was a specialist of unusual ability, silently shook his head as he leaned over the bed and examined the little body with his stethoscope. He said nothing to the family, but after leaving the room, he said to the family physician, "I doubt if this little one will live."

The family doctor had a very tender heart, and knowing that this was the only child, he realized the crushing blow this news would bring to those two loving hearts. He hesitated to tell them, but Mr. Jacobs insisted on having the facts. "We have both agreed, Mr. Jacobs, that your little Betty is in a very serious condition, and she may not live through the night."

The surging of sorrow in the heart of my friend, Mr. Jacobs, overcame him at this point of the story, and he was unable to continue. I sympathized deeply with him and placed my hand on his shoulder in a gesture of affection to assure him of my sympathy in his deep grief. After calming himself, he continued with the story. The little one lived through the night but failed rapidly, and the little life began to slip away, so that as the morning broke the little spirit was taken away. The dark shadows of sorrow fell like an avalanche over the father and the mother, and they seemed utterly helpless in their distress. An undertaker was called, and beautiful little Betty was taken off to be prepared for burial. As the body was taken from the room by the undertakers, Gertrude collapsed and had to be carried to the couch.

Those who have no loving Saviour on whom to lean and no wonderful Lord in whom to trust are not able to stand in the day of the storm, when the winds of adversity beat against the soul and crush the very heart. These two had no one to whom they could go. Friends came in to comfort, but their words seemed to be of no avail. A great dark cloud had entered this home. The sunshine had gone out of their lives. There seemed no hope in sight, and no relief available. Oh! the utter despair when death comes in and there is no Light to dispel and disperse the dark shadows.

Mr. Jacobs turned to me and said, "Dr. Wilson, the world seemed to drop away from beneath me. I was swept off my feet. I was bewildered and perplexed. What could I do? Where could I go? Gertrude's church was closed to her, and mine was closed to me. None of our friends knew God or cared for Him. The sympathy that was brought to us seemed to be hollow mockery. We were in utter despair. Then the day came for the funeral. What should we do?"

When death comes in, peace goes out. When sorrow reigns, there is no rest for the soul or spirit in those who do not know the Lord Jesus Christ. These two friends wanted to find God. They wanted to know His comfort and His solace. They were reaching out into the unknown realm for One whom they had never met and a Saviour whom they had never trusted. They did not know exactly why they could find no remedy, but they knew there was a great aching void with no remedy sufficient to fill it. They sent for the undertaker to come to the home to make the final arrangements for the burial.

Mr. Jacobs continued with his story, "I said to Mr. Morton, the undertaker, 'What shall we do for a service? We do not want to place our little girl in the ground with no word of farewell. We cannot drop that precious little body into the grave with no message of any kind; we bury animals that way, but not our children.'

"Mr. Morton very kindly answered, 'Why do you not ask the rabbi or priest to come?'

"I replied to him, 'These will not come because we do not have an acceptance with them now since we married each other.'

"This answer rather puzzled Mr. Morton, and after pondering the matter for a little while, he said, 'The only remedy I see, Mr. Jacobs, is for you and your dear companion to pray at the graveside yourselves. After your prayers I will pronounce the committal words, and this will close the service.'"

Mr. Jacobs now continued his conversation, saying, "That was a dark hour in my life, Dr. Wilson. The only prayer I knew was one I had learned from my mother when a very little child. Somewhere my wife had learned a little prayer when she was a little girl, which I think began with 'Now I lay me down to sleep.' We knelt together beside the grave after the casket had been lowered, and with our arms around each other, we each one said our little prayer."

Turning to me in his deep sorrow, Mr. Jacobs said, "Dr. Wilson, where is my little girl? Will I ever see her again? Is she in that grave, dead like the animals, or is she living somewhere? Do you think that Gertrude and I will ever see our little Betty again? Do tell me if you know."

The tears were streaming from my own eyes as well as his, and the sadness of this melancholy lonesomeness stirred my soul deeply. When I was able to speak calmly, I replied, "Opinion is divided among Christians in regard to what happens to children when they die. It is my opinion, Mr. Jacobs, that children of the age of your little girl are protected by the sacrifice of Calvary and are under the precious blood that Christ shed. Other Bible scholars are not of this opinion, but I refer you to Matthew 18:11: 'For the Son of Man is come to seek and to save that which was lost.' I believe that this refers to such little girls as yours. Whether it is so or not I cannot definitely say, but I do know that if she went to heaven to be with Christ then it is necessary that you should be saved by this same Saviour. You must trust Him with your soul, and so must Gertrude. He came to save you, Mr. Jacobs. He paid a great price for you at the Cross, and He is the Lamb of God who came to bear away your sins."

I urged my heartbroken friend to believe the gospel messages which I read to him from Isaiah 44:22, Isaiah 53:5, Acts 13:38-39, and 1 Peter 3:18. All of my efforts, however, failed. His great grief seemed to hinder his faith. He was so occupied with his sorrow that he could not see the Saviour. I pleaded with him for some time after seeking to unfold the Scriptures to him, but all to no avail. He shook my hand cordially, thanked me for the sympathy and proffered help, and went out into the busy world again, carrying the load which Christ would have taken from him if he had only permitted Him.

Friend, are you carrying a burden and a load? The Saviour came to bear your sins, carry your sorrows, and give you rest. Will you not come to Him for that priceless blessing (Isaiah 53:4-6)?

Are You Bad Enough to Go to Hell?

On the particular morning when the events of this story transpired, my heart was unusually happy because of a new revelation which the Holy Spirit had given me of Himself on the previous evening. Upon leaving home for the office, I asked the Holy Spirit for the privilege of being His channel that day, so that some heart might be reached by His message and brought to the Lord Jesus Christ.

About ten o'clock, two young ladies entered the office, soliciting advertising for a national magazine. I had often given these friends some business and was now ready for another contract, as they knew. At my invitation, they seated themselves at my desk, one just across the table from me and the other at my left. Having transacted our business with regard to the advertising contract and having closed the arrangement, I said to them, "Girls, are you both saved, or are you lost girls on the way to a lost eternity?"

This unusual question greatly surprised both of them. The one sitting opposite me, Miss D————, became quite serious at once. Her sister, at my left, thought it was a great joke and expressed her feelings by a rather loud outburst of laughter, which was heard throughout the office.

Miss S————, who was seated at my left, was quite sure that someone had been telling me wrong things about herself and her sister. She hastened to assure me that they were both very lovely girls. They taught Sunday school classes in the same church, were raised by a good Christian mother, and never did anything wrong. The older girl, Miss D————, was not quite so sure. She said, "Doctor, I was up last evening until quite late, reading my Bible and wondering if I had everything for salvation that I should have. I do not feel at all happy about my condition and would be so glad if you could give me any help."

Opening my Bible to John 3:16, I handed it to Miss D———— and said, "Will you please read this verse slowly and aloud?"

She did so and added, "I know that verse well and have always believed it."

"But you still feel, do you not, Miss D————, that you are perishing and are still lost?"

"Yes, I do," she answered, "and yet I do not understand why, when I believe all of the Bible."

"It is because you have believed the facts, but this belief has not led you to accept God's gift of His Son. Why do you not take Christ just now? He is the One who will save you from perishing. He will save you this moment, if you will take Him and make Him, just now, your own Lord and Saviour. Will you trust Him with your soul?"

The heart of the young lady responded immediately to the call, and with a glad heart she accepted the Saviour, offering her hand to me across the desk in evidence of her sincerity.

Turning to her sister, I said, "Miss S————, it is quite evident that you do *not* believe the Bible."

"I certainly do," she replied, "every word of it."

"I want you to read this passage in Romans 3:9-19 and tell me whether this description is true of you."

She read it clear through from my Bible which I had handed her and said emphatically, "No, sir, indeed it is not true of me; I am not that kind of a woman."

"Very well," said I, "take these scissors"—and I handed her mine—"and cut this passage out of the Bible, for I do not want anything in my Bible that is not true."

Miss D————, who had trusted the Saviour, spoke to her sister and said, "Sister, you know that you are as bad as that. God always speaks the truth, and you should acknowledge it."

"I know better," she replied, "I have not lived that kind of a life at all."

Interposing in the conversation, I said to Miss S————, "This is not a description of your *deeds;* it is a record of what God sees in your heart."

"I reject it," she answered, "and will not believe that I am as bad as that. I will not cut it out of the Bible, however, for it certainly is true of some folks that I know."

"Perhaps, Miss S————, we can find some other passage in the Bible that *is* true of you. Please read this portion in Mark 7:21-23 and tell me whether you think those thirteen things describe your heart correctly."

When she came to verse 23 and read, "All these evil things come from within and defile the man," she spoke rather forcefully and said, "No sir, most of these things are not true of me, but the last two things are, for I know that both pride and foolishness are often in my life."

Upon hearing this partial confession, I handed Miss S———— a lead pencil, and said, "Will you please write at the end of verse 23, 'All but Miss S————'? Since you say that all of these things do not come out of *your* heart, we should revise the Bible to make it tell the truth. If you wish, you can write in the margin of my Bible, 'Only the last two things come out of my heart.'"

This suggestion did not please Miss S———— at all. She rather resented it and said, "God wrote the Bible the way He wanted it. I certainly will not presume to add any words to it. These verses may be true of many wicked people, but I tell you again that I do not like that kind of a wicked life."

It was quite evident now that the passages concerning outrageous sins would not appeal to her at all, so I suggested that we turn to another passage and see whether this one might fit her case. The portion turned to was Matthew

13:18-23, 36-42. She read the passages aloud, and I asked her whether she belonged to the wheat or to the tares. "The tares," I explained, "are plants which look very much like the wheat, resemble the wheat in every respect, grow right in with the wheat, and yet they are not wheat at all, but only hypocrites. No wheat grains are found in the pods on the bearded head. The ordinary person thinks that the tares are wheat, but the expert farmer knows that the tares are fit only for the burning. Which of these are you, Miss S————?"

Lying on her lap was a large, brown fur piece, upon which I saw beaded tears drop. Her head was bowed so that her face could not be seen, but the tears told the story of a heart touched by the power of God and convicted of its need.

"That is a picture of me," she finally said with sobs. "I have kept up this hypocrisy long enough. I might as well confess what I know to be true in my heart. I have been religious, but I have never been saved. I have been active in the church but never had peace in my soul. God ought to punish me, for I have been such a hypocrite."

Conviction of sin, when it is of this character, is soon followed by salvation when the gospel is properly presented. Miss D———— saw the sorrow of heart which Miss S———— exhibited and said to her, "Sister, why do you not accept the Lord Jesus as I have? I know He has saved me, for He died for me, and I have trusted Him. Will you not trust Him as I have?"

"Yes, Miss S————," I added, "He calls you and says, 'Come unto me, all ye that labor and are heavy laden, and I will give you rest' (Matt. 11:28). He said to one woman, 'Thy sins are forgiven' (Luke 7:48). He will give you that assurance too, Miss S————, if you will just now acknowledge your need and accept Him and His finished work on the Cross. He died for you there, paid the price, bore your sins, took your punishment, and now wants to give you Himself and all the blessed fruits of that wonderful work of Calvary."

"I believe it," she said. "I do accept Him. All along I thought it was religion that I needed, but I never could get any peace in my Christian work and religious services. Of course I could not. I see clearly now that what I needed was the Lord Jesus, and I am so glad I can take Him and know that He blots out all of my sins today."

The two sisters left the office with happy hearts. They were now sisters in the faith, as well as sisters in the flesh. They followed the Lord in baptism shortly afterwards that they might go all the way with Him.

Are you only a professing Christian, or have you accepted the Saviour and received from Him the gift of eternal life? Do not let Satan deceive you. Do not miss a meeting with the Lord Jesus Christ.

This Clerk Took Inventory

I shall tell you the story of a sudden transformation which took place in the heart of a young lady at the notion counter of a large department store.

It was my privilege to be preaching in an eastern city near the Christmas holidays. I entered this great department store in order to purchase some presents for the dear ones at home. There was no information desk near the front door, and therefore I stepped over to the counter to make inquiry of the young lady concerning the department where I might find the articles I wished to purchase. The clerk was very amiable and kind. She was placing some figures on a ruled chart that lay before her on the counter.

I waited a few minutes until she would look up, for I did not wish to disturb her work, especially since I did not intend to purchase anything from her. My presence near her was noted in a few minutes, and the young lady looked up with a smile and said, "May I do something for you, sir?" I replied, "Yes, I would like to be directed to the department where I will find such and such an article for sale." She was quite willing to give me the information and did give me the instructions that would lead me to the proper counter on the third floor of the building.

I apologized to her for stopping her work and said, "Are you taking inventory today?" She replied, "No, sir, I am just preparing my sheets and am entering the names of the articles I sell in order that I may be ready when we do take inventory. We take inventory on Sunday because on that day the doors are locked and we are not bothered with customers." At once the Spirit suggested to me that here was a probable prospect for heaven. I acted upon the suggestion at once and said to her, "Are you not sorry to miss the church services on Sunday?"

"Yes," she replied, "I am sorry, but of course when I am working for the company I must do what they say. When they select Sunday for inventory then I have to stay here and take it."

"My, but I am sorry that is the case," I said. "Tell me, little lady, did you ever take inventory of yourself?"

The expression of her face was most interesting. She gazed at me in a rather peculiar way and did not reply for a moment because of the shock of the question. Her answer was deliberately but calmly given; she said, "Yes, mister, rather frequently I take inventory of myself, but it isn't a pleasant job because I always come out on the wrong side. I do not know why it is, but I simply cannot be as good as I know I should be."

I saw at once that here was another heart which had been touched by the Spirit of God through some of the past years and that He had left in that soul some realization of a need and a lack. She did not know what it was, but she did know that she fell far short of God's requirements.

This was such a splendid opportunity that I immediately laid aside the thought of going upstairs for a purchase in order that I might seek to win this friend for our blessed Lord. I leaned over on the glass case with my Bible in my hand and said to her, "My friend, there is a way for you to change that record and present to God an inventory that is absolutely perfect and one that He will gladly accept. How would you like to present to God a perfectly sinless life?"

A gleam of hope appeared in her face, followed by shadows of despair. "There is no use my trying that," she said, "I have tried my best to be a Christian and found that it simply will not work. Every time I take inventory and

see how bad the record is I am determined to live a different
life and to be what I should be. It just isn't of any use.
I cannot be good, not even as good as I want to be, let
alone as good as God says I should be."

I was touched by the earnestness of this young lady.
She was really exercised about the matter and was not a
careless listener. It was a joy to watch her face as thoughts
flooded her soul, thoughts of her failures and thoughts of
God's holy demands. I said to her, "My friend, you may
have a perfect life even now to present to God. God has
made it possible for you to get rid of all of your sin-stains,
the faults and the failures, and to have a record in heaven
of perfect righteousness, one which meets all of God's
requirements."

She came back at me at once with this statement, "Mister,
you do not know me. If you knew me, you never would
say anything like that. I simply cannot live as I should. I
cannot resist the call to sin. Some way or other my resolutions
disappear when the right kind of temptation comes. Please
do not make fun of me by telling me that I can live right
when I know that I cannot."

"You are quite mistaken, my friend; you did not really
understand clearly my message to you, and perhaps I did
not make it plain. I did not say that you could LIVE a life
that would be acceptable to God, but I did say that you
could HAVE a life that is so blameless and so pure that
God will accept it from you and give you a place in glory
with Him."

This interested my friend deeply, although I could see
that she did not believe a word of it. She had never heard
of the righteousness that I was referring to. It was all a mystery
to her, and her mind was darkness itself. "Let me explain
to you," I continued. "God has provided for you a godly
life which you did not live, a righteousness that you cannot
make, a holiness that is absolutely pure, and this wonderful
blessing may be yours this morning right here behind the
counter in the store."

The astonishment of this young lady was greatly increased by this statement, and she answered quickly and with some feeling, "I never heard of such a thing. How can anybody be righteous unless they live that way? How can anybody be good when they are not good? I don't understand you at all. This is the strangest thing I have ever heard."

I now opened my Bible and read to her Romans 4:6: "'David also describeth the blessedness of the man unto whom God imputeth righteousness without works.' You see, little lady, the Lord does have a righteousness for us which you may have without working for it. It is God's righteousness obtained because Christ lived a sinless life and died a sufficient death. If you will just now trust this lovely Lord Jesus, God in heaven will give to you the perfectly beautiful, sinless, stainless life of the Lord Jesus Christ. He will reckon your sinfulness to the Saviour and His righteousness to you. Christ takes your place. Christ was made sin for you that you might be made the righteousness of God in Him" (2 Cor. 5:21).

My friend listened very attentively. There was no resentment there. There was no resistance toward my effort and no repudiating of my message. She continued to listen quietly, saying nothing. I took advantage of this lovely attitude and said further, "May I give you another illustration of this blessed truth? Suppose that you were a very poor girl, receiving small wages and helping to support an aged mother. You lived a beautiful life. You were attractive in your personality. Your poverty had not led you away from the path of rectitude, but your life was above blame.

"Now suppose, further, that some very wealthy man would come along, a man worth millions of dollars in cash with a beautiful mansion and everything your heart could wish. He would happen by chance to purchase something from you and would be attracted by your graces. Now remember you are very poor and he is very rich. Your charm attracts this wealthy gentleman, and he proposes that you would become his life companion. This proposal you accept most gladly. It seems too good to be true and too wonderful.

"Suppose now that the papers tomorrow morning come out with the pictures of both of you taken at the wedding and with the announcement that you had become his wife. Tell me, my friend, would you not at once be a millionaire? Could you not go into the society where he is welcome and there find yourself quite welcome? Would you not have unlimited credit at the stores so that you could purchase expensive jewelry, fine furs, and silk dresses and have them charged to his account?"

The clerk saw the logic of this, of course, and at once agreed that she would be all of this because of the standing of her husband. She would have imputed riches, imputed social standing, imputed credit at the stores. She would have this because she belonged to him.

I now applied this truth to her own heart and said, "It is the same way with our blessed Lord. The moment you trust the Son of God, the Father will impute to you the glories, the beauties, and the perfection of His Son. You will be in God's family because you belong to His Son. You can go where He goes because you are His own. Then when you take inventory you will not look at your righteousness at all, but at the merits and perfections of the One you have married, or trusted, the perfect Lord Jesus Christ" (Rom. 4:5-7).

It was as though the sun had shined into the darkness and the darkness did comprehend it. She saw for the first time how she could take inventory and find Christ dwelling in the soul and have perfect peace and rest. What a joy it was to show this precious soul the gospel of God's rich grace and to bring her to a saving trust in Christ Jesus the Lord.

It may be that the reader of this story is in a similar position. Let me say to you freely that you may have Christ Jesus also, and He will give you the righteousness of God.

The Candlestick Was Not in the Ark

During the winter months, I had the privilege of teaching a Bible class of pastors who requested some messages on how to find Christ and the gospel in the Old Testament. It was an interesting class, and the men seemed to appreciate very much the help received in regard to the types and shadows found in the messages of the prophets. During the course of the lessons, we came to a discussion of the seven articles of furniture in the Jewish tabernacle.

The wonderful pictures of Christ seen in the various parts of the tabernacle filled the hearts of these preachers with new joy. Among the things discussed was the ark of the covenant found in the holy of holies behind the veil. This ark with the mercy seat upon its top presented many beautiful pictures of the Lord Jesus in His deity, His humanity, and His sacrifice. I asked the question, "What was in the ark of the covenant? Who knows?" There was a long pause, and no one seemed ready to answer. Finally the pastor of a large, well-known church arose, and said, "Since none of the other brethren seem willing to venture a guess, I will suggest that possibly the candlestick was in the ark." His reply was received with silence by the other members of the class. They did not know whether his answer was correct or not.

The ignorance which was displayed by this reply rather startled me, and it was with some difficulty that I restrained

my feelings of amusement. An explanation was immediately
given to the men, in which I called their attention to the
fact that the candlestick was probably larger than the ark
and was located in the holy place on the outside of the veil
and separated from the ark by the veil. We also observed
that the purpose of the candlestick was to give light throughout the holy place, so that the priests could go about their
service in attending to the altar of incense and the table of
shewbread. This purpose could not be served if the candlestick had been inside the ark and covered over with the
mercy seat.

At the close of the class, there was quite a discussion
about how little had been taught in the seminary with regard
to the meanings of the figures, types, and shadows of the
Old Testament economy. A few days after this peculiar incident occurred, I was visited by this pastor who had made
the peculiar reply, and he informed me that he had come
to my office to find Christ. "Do you know," he said, "that
after leaving the class the other day, I went home to my
study and thought over the ridiculous answer that I had given
to your question. It occurred to me that perhaps I was just
as ignorant on other matters in the Bible. I started to give
myself an examination on my own state and condition before
God. I wrote down the questions on a sheet of paper and
then wrote out the answers, as I subjected my soul to a
thorough test. I was really alarmed at my ignorance of things
which should be of prime importance. I came to the conclusion that I had had quite a religious experience without really
meeting the Saviour and receiving eternal life from Him."

I looked at the gentleman in amazement. I could see
that his heart had been deeply touched by his condition and
that his soul was filled with hunger for the truth of God
and the light of Christ. He continued his story, saying, "How
I ever got through the seminary and these several years of
preaching without having eternal life, I cannot understand.
I can see now that I learned only the mechanics of Christianity and have never felt the life-giving touch of the Lord Himself. I learned the theory; I embraced the theology; but now

I want the Lord Himself. Do tell me how to meet Jesus Christ."

My heart was deeply touched by this appeal. The Holy Spirit had used that strange incident concerning the candlestick to reveal to my friend the darkness of his heart and the need of his soul. What a wonder-working Person He is! What peculiar methods are used by Him for reaching hearts! Who would ever have thought of reaching the heart of this well-known and much-loved preacher through such an obscure passage as the one in Exodus concerning the candlestick and the ark? The Holy Spirit is sovereign and may use any part of His own Word to bring about His own results in His own way.

Soulwinners should let the Spirit of God fill their hearts and minds with all the Word, from Genesis to Revelation, that the soul can absorb. They should not confine their ministry to a few gospel verses. Every part of the Scripture has life in it and is profitable for man's heart and mind. What part of the Word should I use with this pastor? The question was running over and over in my mind as he sat there telling me his story. I sought to diagnose his case as he talked with me and finally decided that he had learned the facts without appropriating them for his own heart. He had learned that the Lord Jesus came to save men but had missed applying that salvation to himself.

I asked my friend when he had received the Lord Jesus as his own personal Saviour. "Have you really had a personal meeting with Christ, or did you just decide to live a Christian life and enter the ministry as a means of bringing blessing to others and of making a living for yourself?"

"Really, Doctor," he said, "as I have examined my life in the last few days, I am convinced that such a meeting never took place. Christ has been to me a wonderful, historical character, a pattern of good men, the Son of God, the Saviour of sinners; but I have never yet met Him face to face, confessed to Him my need, and made Him my own Lord."

"Have you noticed John 1:12?" I asked. "It reads like this: 'But as many as received him, to them gave he power to become the sons of God, even to them that believe on his name.'" The preacher saw immediately the simplicity and the beauty of belonging to Jesus Christ personally and at once accepted Him. The gift of Jesus Christ became a reality in his soul, and the peace of God filled his heart. I followed this Scripture with another found in 1 John 5:12: "He that hath the Son hath life; and he that hath not the Son of God hath not life." I read the passage to him slowly and with some emphasis on the word *hath.* He saw the point readily, and his faith was strengthened. "Yes, I see the point clearly, Dr. Wilson," he said. "Christ is my own now. I have met Him today, and He has become my Lord and Saviour. Thank you so much for showing me the way to Him."

Have you, dear reader, personally made Christ Jesus your own? Have you met Him for yourself? Do you enjoy that blessed experience today?

The Intern Was Surprised

In one of our great hospitals, there worked a fine young man of about thirty years of age as an intern. He had only recently graduated from an eastern school of medicine. His parents were missionaries in China but had left the young man at home, after arranging a course of education for him in college and in medicine. They were anticipating his return to them on the mission field to labor as the Lord's servant after his graduation.

The faith which the young man professed was the faith of his parents and not his own. When he entered college, he found that this faith was considered out-of-date. Those in the social circles of the college did not desire his type of Christianity, nor was any conversation on this subject agreeable to his companions. The arguments of infidels and atheists, together with the sneers and the jeers of his associates, soon robbed him of the religion which he inherited from his devoted parents. Not many months after he had matriculated, he renounced all religious faith and became indifferent to his former confession.

During the four years of his college education and another four years of medical training, he had drifted farther and farther into ways of worldliness and paths of sin. There was no restraining influence in his life; no one cared for his soul. His fellow students had no interest in his spiritual welfare; everything about him tended to drive him farther and farther from the Lord. What a tragedy it is that those who are invited into the very heart-secrets of the family pay so little attention to the welfare of their own souls! An atmosphere of godlessness pervades the halls of most medical institutions, and on commencement day the doctor leaves the college trained in medicine but practically abandoned to a life in which God and His claims are not recognized. This was the experience of the intern portrayed in this story.

One summer morning, while praying about the matters of the day, I sought the counsel of the Holy Spirit in directing my path and asked Him to make the contacts which would bring glory to the Lord. It was necessary that I spend part of the morning in the operating room at the hospital heretofore mentioned. We made preparation for the operation in the surgeon's dressing room, scrubbing the hands and donning the white suits which were worn on such occasions. The conversation turned to the things of God, and I had the privilege of directing the attention of both the surgeons and the interns present to the Cross of Calvary. It was only a short ministry, for the patients from the wards were being brought to the operating room and had to be cared for immediately.

Several days elapsed, in consequence of which I had practically forgotten the incident in the dressing room. While I was seated in my study, the telephone rang, and a voice said, "Doctor, I would like very much to come out and have a personal interview with you."

"Who is it?" I inquired.

"It is Dr. ————," he answered. "I am one of the interns at the hospital. I was in the dressing room the other morning when you were talking about our responsibility to God, and it is concerning that matter that I wish this interview."

I assured him that he would be quite welcome and made a four o'clock appointment for the afternoon, when he would be free from his duties at the hospital.

My young doctor friend was a fine specimen of manhood. He was a tall, erect, and well-poised gentleman, and one could readily detect the culture and the splendid training he had gained through the years at college. He seemed tremendously in earnest as he seated himself beside my desk.

"Do you know my father and mother?" he asked. "They are missionaries in China, and their names have appeared rather frequently in the press for meritorious services."

I expressed my sorrow as I told him that I had not had the privilege of knowing his parents, nor of reading about them.

"They were very godly folks," he continued. "They taught me the Bible, prayed with me ever since I can remember, and sought to bring me up as a Christian boy, until they went to China."

As the thought of his former habits, compared with his present life, crowded his memory, emotion overwhelmed his heart for the moment, and he remained silent. I refrained from interrupting as he regained his composure. Resuming his story, he said, "When the folks left for China, I entered college as they had instructed and arranged, fully intending to prepare myself for the work of a medical missionary. It was not long until I realized that I was not rooted and grounded in the truths my parents had taught me. The things I once held dear gradually slipped from my grasp, until I abandoned myself to a life of unbelief and sin. Father soon discovered from my letters that I was not going on well, and after more than a year, I finally unburdened to him the whole truth. This nearly broke the hearts of Father and Mother, for it never occurred to them that their boy would become an enemy of God and a lover of the ways of the world. They began at once to tell me in their letters how they were praying for me, gave me passage after passage from the Scriptures, and sought to turn me back to Christianity. This rather angered me. I determined more than ever that I would not be tied to their apron strings."

"Tell me, Doctor," I asked, "what has happened in your life that brings about your present desire to know the Lord?"

"The death of my mother," he replied quickly. "I did not know that she was ill. In fact, she became sick very

suddenly and died before help could be obtained. It hurts
my heart deeply to think that Mother passed away knowing
that the son of her love was a wayward wanderer, living
for the devil. Father's letter told me of her prayers for me
right up to the end. It is not right that I should continue
as I am. I must get to God. I must get rid of these habits
that are wrecking my life. I have come to you to ascertain
how it may be done."

Taking my Bible from the desk, I turned to Luke 19:10.
"Here, Dr. ————, is a message which I believe will be
a blessing to your heart."

He leaned over toward the desk, and we read the verse
together: "The Son of man is come to seek and to save that
which was lost."

"There is a Saviour for you. It is Jesus. He came to
seek you and to save you. He alone can break the power
of sin. He only can conquer Satan. He is the life-giver. It
is through His blood that you may be forgiven."

"Yes, Doctor, I know it," he said, "but I used to profess
to be a Christian and turned my back on it. Do you think
that God would take me back again after treating Him as
I have done?"

"Yes," I answered. "The father took the prodigal son
when he returned. The Lord welcomed Naomi when she
came back from Moab. He will welcome you and will save
you, if you, too, will turn to Him with your whole heart
and will accept the Lord Jesus Christ."

With drooped head, my friend was soon lost in meditation as he thought over the past life, the lost opportunities,
the mother who had died with a broken heart, the father
whose hopes and ambitions for his son had been blasted.
He was considering also the price that he must pay should
he make a decision for the Saviour. He would be exposed
to the sneers and the jeers of those whose lives were given
over to personal gain and sinful satisfaction. As he meditated,
I prayed, asking the Holy Spirit to do His good work in
this troubled heart. I knew that only He could reveal Christ

to this man and bring peace through the saving power of Jesus Christ.

The young doctor weighed the case from every angle. He thought of what the future held. He knew that judgment and condemnation lay at the end of the road that he was traveling. Knowing, too, that he was lost and that Satan was his master, he trembled at the thought of meeting an angry God, after all the opportunities he had neglected. Suddenly he looked up and with intense earnestness said, "If you will show me how to come to Christ, I will come right now. I am ready to pay the price. I am ready to be a Christian out-and-out. What shall I do?"

I turned to John 3:16 and read the passage aloud and quite slowly: " 'For God so loved the world, that he gave his only begotten Son, that whosoever believeth in him should not perish, but have everlasting life.' God has given Christ to you, Doctor. It is your privilege to accept that gift. Christ will save you. He will blot out your sins. He will write your name in the book of life. No one else can do it. God has given Christ to you. Will you take the gift just now? Will you tell God that you do accept His Son?"

"Yes," he replied, "I will do so at once."

He knelt beside the wicker chair near my desk, and I knelt also with him, as he poured out his heart to God in thanksgiving and praise.

I was struck with the note of thanksgiving in his prayer, when he said, "I did not know, God, that You were so good. I did not think that You would let me come back to You after treating You as I have. I thank You for sending Jesus Christ to save me. I accept Him as Your gift to me. I believe He died for me and has blotted out my sins."

As we arose to our feet, he remarked, "I must send word at once to my father. How glad he will be to know that his prayers and Mother's tears have not been unavailing! How I do wish that Mother had lived to see and know that I have been saved! I wonder if God took my mother away to bring me to my senses. What a terrible price to pay! How the Lord must have loved me to follow me up as He has and to love me so freely!"

The doctor returned to the hospital, resumed his duties as an intern, and at the close of the year left the city to serve the Lord in his chosen field. The parents prayed in China; the Lord answered in Kansas City. The Holy Spirit knows neither time nor distance. He works out the will of God and reaches hearts in His own blessed way. How we should wait on Him more often to do His blessed work in the lives of those we love!

The Nurse Wanted Christ, Too

The pastor of the church in which I was holding services on one occasion requested me to accompany him as he went to visit one of the members of his congregation, who was ill in a large hospital. It is always a pleasure for me to visit sick folks. My medical training has given me a love for the work of tending to the suffering, and so I was happy to grant his request. Shortly afterwards we arrived at the hospital.

The gentleman who was sick had been injured in an automobile accident, and quite seriously so. He had been in the sickroom for several weeks and was attended by a most amiable nurse, a Swedish lady about forty years of age.

This friend was rather popular in the church and had had many visitors who came to encourage his heart, bring flowers with which to brighten the room, and minister words of comfort from the Scriptures. The pastor had often called, and so had some of the Sunday school teachers with whom he was associated in his Sunday school activities. They had been delightfully helpful to him, and he had thanked God for their coming.

As the pastor and I entered the room, we received a cordial greeting from our friend, who was now recovering rather rapidly. We found him sitting in a wheelchair with his Bible on a nearby stand and a tray on which was his lunch, partly eaten. The pastor introduced me, and we were soon happily engaged in conversation about the wonderful ways of God in permitting trouble and then providing a remedy. I mentioned to him that, in my judgment, it was a greater miracle to keep the suffering soul in happy peace and sweet contentment than it was to calm the storm of trouble surging around him. This seemed to be a new thought to him, and he thanked the Lord that this had been his blessed portion all through the accident and its unhappy results.

While we were conversing together, the nurse stood over near the dresser, on which were the medicines, bandages, and a vase of beautiful flowers.

I have always had a deep interest in the welfare of nurses, for they are such self-sacrificing friends, doing the most difficult things without murmuring or complaining, serving any hour of the day or night without faultfinding, and always bringing a sweet, happy smile into the shadows of the sick room.

I stepped over to the nurse and said, "Your patient has a great many Christian visitors, doesn't he?"

"Yes," she answered, "his friends are very faithful to visit him, and they do tell him some wonderfully interesting things out of the Bible."

"Do any of these friends bring any message of comfort to you for your heart, Nurse?" I inquired.

Her eyes moistened, and she said with some feeling, "No, none of them has anything to say to me. You see, I am not a Christian, and they come to talk to this man who is a Christian."

The pastor was listening intently to our conversation. These words of accusation by the nurse brought a feeling a sorrow and shame to this lovely man of God, who really was a true servant of God but who had failed to observe the need of the nurse in the room with his Christian friend. He said nothing, however, but listened for the further remarks between us.

"I am very sorry, Nurse," I said, "that those splendid Christians who have been coming here have overlooked you, but I am very glad to tell you that the Lord Jesus did not overlook you. He remembered you at Calvary, and He remembers you now while He is on the throne in glory. He loved you then, and He loves you now. He came to save you just as much as He came to save this patient of yours. Perhaps He permitted the other friends to pass you by in order that He might give me the honor and the privilege of telling you of the Great Physician who loves to save nurses."

By this time the tears were flowing freely. All unknown to those who had visited the sick man, this nurse had been listening, the hunger had been increasing, and the desire to have what they were talking about became more and more acute in her soul. "One soweth and another reapeth" was the statement of our blessed Lord about the ministry in the harvest field. It is still true. Although the visiting Christians had overlooked this splendid prospect, nevertheless God used their words to prepare her heart for the message which I was to have the joy of bringing.

I took my Bible from my pocket and began to read to her Luke 19:10: " 'The Son of Man is come to seek and to save that which was lost.' Are you lost, Nurse?" I inquired kindly.

She replied, "I suppose I am, Doctor, because I do not have the experience that these folks have been talking about, and I do not seem to know Christ in the way they do. Will you help me to understand?"

"Yes, Nurse, I am happy to do so, for I have had the joy of helping other nurses to find the Saviour, and I am sure that you and I may go together to Him and that we shall find Him ready to receive and welcome you. God sent the Saviour to do for you what no one else could do. Your sins need to be put away, whether they be many or few; you need the gift of eternal life; you need your name written in the Lamb's Book of Life; you need to be brought out of Satan's family into God's family by the new birth. All of this the Lord Jesus does as you listen to the message of the Holy Spirit in His precious Word. You turn your case over to the Lord Jesus somewhat in the same way that the patient turns her case over to the physician or as the drowning man turns his case over to the lifeguard. You can do nothing to save yourself, but the Lord Jesus can do everything. If you will accept Him just now, believe that He is the One whom you should trust, and turn your case over to Him, He will accept you immediately and will do all these blessed things that you are in need of today. Will you trust Him?"

The deep agitation of the heart of this nurse was quite evident as she trembled with emotion and sought to conceal the tears that would not stop. She shook her head to confirm her faith, reached out her hand for the grasp of a friend, and then said quietly, "Yes, I will accept Christ Jesus. I would have done so long ago if any of these visiting Christians had wanted me to do so. None of them ever asked me. They did not seem to think that I would care to hear their story, but my heart did want to hear it. I am so glad that God sent a doctor here who really cared for the nurse. You have brought me the gospel, and now the Lord Jesus is mine."

May I urge upon the saints of God that each one of us should be careful not to overlook any possible subject for God's grace. The hungry heart may be quite close to us but may be all unobserved because we are not looking for the troubled soul. What an opportunity was lost by the visitors who came to see the sick man. Any one of them might have won this nurse for the Saviour and thus added to the blessed reward, but none of them was interested in her; they were only interested in the Christian friend. May the God of all grace stir our hearts to want to be like Christ in that we are always seeking for hearts for God.

A Darkened Heart Surrounded by Light

Some years ago a great movement was inaugurated in this country and was termed "the Interchurch World Movement." Their headquarters were in the old Siegel-Cooper Building, New York, which was of unusual size and capable of accommodating a large army of workers.

As I was riding along in the subway, reading the *New York Times,* I noticed an article in which it was reported that the office of this company in the Siegel-Cooper Building was considering the purchase of tents to be used in the harvest fields of Nebraska, Kansas, and Oklahoma. In these tents religious meetings were to be held at night and social accommodations offered for other times.

Being interested in this movement, I went to the purchasing department to make inquiry about the situation. Here I was met by a young lady about twenty-six years of age who expressed regret that the party that should be seen was out of the building. Since I could not come again that day, I suggested that I would return in about two days. She advised me that no doubt he would be glad to see me then.

The young woman was indeed quite pleasant, seemed greatly interested in the work she was doing, and was delightfully enthusiastic over the progress being made by the various departments in that huge institution. She asked me whether or not I was familiar with the operations of the various departments and the results that were being obtained.

Upon receiving a negative reply, she at once began to explain the workings of the art department, the map section, the social service plans, and other divisions of the enterprise. Addressing her, I said, "Do you suppose that this great army of people will be like Noah's carpenters?"

"I was not aware that Noah had any carpenters," she replied.

"Neither am I sure that he had them," I said, "but he must have had help in building that great ship, and it is quite certain that all of those helpers, except his own three sons, refused to go into the ark and were drowned. Do you think that these friends on the floor where you work, including yourself, might possibly be like those men? You and the others here are working earnestly to bring the gospel and the way of salvation to millions of lost souls scattered throughout the world. Have these been saved who are doing this work, and have you been saved yourself?"

The young woman looked quite surprised and, in her astonishment, said, "Why, no, I am sure I have never been saved, and I have not heard anyone among the hundreds on this floor say he was saved. What do you mean by being saved?"

"To be saved," I assured her, "is to know that the Lord Jesus has put your sins away by His work at Calvary, has written your name in the Book of Life as one of His own children, and has given you the gift of eternal life which entitles you to a place in heaven. Has this happened to you?"

"No, it has not," she answered; "I have never heard of it before."

"Do you not go to church?" she was asked.

"Yes, I am in a Sunday school class of twenty-four girls about my own age, but the teacher has never told us of this. I never heard it before. Is there anything more in the Bible like this story of Noah?"

Noting the honest heart and the deep interest of this young life, I took out my Bible and read to her Romans 10:1-3: "Brethren, my heart's desire and prayer to God for Israel is, that they might be saved. For I bear them record that they have a zeal of God, but not according to knowledge. For they being ignorant of *God's righteousness*, and going about to establish their own righteousness, have not submitted themselves unto the *righteousness of God*."

"You will see from this Scripture," I explained, "that there are two kinds of righteousness. One kind is called 'God's,' and the other kind is called 'yours.' You have been striving evidently to make a righteousness by being good, going to church, keeping out of sinful practices, and in various ways endeavoring to live a good life."

Just at this point, a gentleman came and called for the young lady, so that it was necessary for me to say, "I will be back Wednesday to see the purchasing agent." During those intervening hours, I prayed earnestly that the gentleman would not be in when I returned, so that the conversation with the young lady might be resumed. Others were asked to pray also.

Wednesday morning at ten o'clock, I again entered the great office on the fourth floor. The young lady was watching for me and hurried across the floor to meet me in the center of the room. "The gentleman you came to see is not in this morning. I am sorry, but he has been delayed. Really, sir, I am rather glad he is not here, for since our conversation last Monday, I have had no peace in my heart. My appetite has gone, and I have been unable to sleep with comfort. I see that I am lost and on the outside of the door, and I *do* want you to tell me how to escape the terrible wrath of God which must come upon me for my sins."

Immediately I turned to John 5:24 and read, "Verily, verily, I say unto you, He that heareth my word, and believeth on him that sent me, hath everlasting life, and shall not come into condemnation [judgment]; but is passed from death unto life."

"Christ is God's ark of safety for the sinner today. You may come to Him with your guilt and sin just as you are, and just now, here in this office, the Saviour will accept you, for that is His work. He loves to forgive. God has sent Him to save. He is waiting for you to present yourself to

Him and thus prove that you believe in Him as the One whom God has sent to save you." Thus I explained the passage.

"But will I be saved if I take Christ just now and give myself to Him?"

Seeking wisdom, I turned to Acts 13:38-39: "Be it known unto you therefore, men and brethren, that through this man is preached unto you the forgiveness of sins; and by him all that believe are justified from all things, from which ye could not be justified by the law of Moses."

"Here God Himself assures you that forgiveness of sins and justification are yours the moment you believe in Christ Jesus. Will you now take Him, believe in Him, and trust Him with your soul?"

Extending her hand to me, she said with tears, "Yes, I do believe in Him. I never saw it in that way before. I am so glad that today I may enter into that ark. I do enter in; I do trust Christ Jesus now."

The Lord enable each one who reads this story to do likewise and thus be safe from coming wrath.

From the Parlor to the Kitchen

Mr. Manchester was not altogether happy in his home life. He and his wife were at odds with each other about religion. He had been taught that the Lord Jesus Christ puts away all the sins of the sinner when he trusts Him with his soul. His wife would not agree at all with this position. She had been raised to believe that salvation was to be earned by good works, faithful attendance at church, and holding out faithful to the end of life. They had many arguments on this subject, and it disrupted the home in a way that made both of them very unhappy and kept them from having sweet fellowship together. Mr. Manchester confided in me that this problem was hindering the peace of their hearts, neither one of them was satisfied, and the home was on the verge of breaking up.

I was invited to come to that home for supper one evening. My friend asked me to bring up the subject somehow in an indirect way and in such a way that his wife would not think that he had been putting me up to some trick in order to catch her unawares and start an argument. I assured him that I would be very careful about this matter and would not give an offense to this wife by finding fault with her.

I went a little early to supper in order to have a visit before the meal, for it was necessary for me to leave shortly afterwards, and therefore we must have our visit early. I was led into the parlor by Mr. Manchester, for the wife was in the kitchen preparing the meal. He whispered to me that it might be helpful if my talk with him would be loud enough so that she could hear it in the kitchen but without being seen. We began at once to talk about the things concerning the loveliness of Christ and His power to save. We considered together Isaiah 44:22, in which we read, "I have blotted out, as a thick cloud, thy transgressions, and as a cloud thy sins: return unto me; for I have redeemed thee." We were impressed by the fact that He did not say that part of the sins were blotted out. We noticed that the passage did not say that they were blotted out up to a certain place in our lives. I called the attention of my host to the fact that if the Saviour did not blot out all the sins from the cradle to the grave when He died on the Cross, then it would be necessary for Christ to return and die again for the sins that were omitted at Calvary. He agreed with me heartily and mentioned that he had not thought of that angle of salvation, though he had been convinced some years before that the Saviour finished the work and that there was no need for Him to return and to suffer again.

We noticed together the New Testament passage on the same subject. It is found in Colossians 2:14 and proclaims the same truth as the one in the Old Testament. We read the passage aloud, loud enough so the wife in the kitchen could hear: "And you, being dead in your sins and the uncircumcision of your flesh, hath he quickened together with him, having forgiven you all trespasses; blotting out the handwriting of ordinances that was against us, which was contrary to us, and took it out of the way, nailing it to his cross." We agreed together on the meaning of the passage, i.e., that *all* the trespasses were blotted out, *all* the broken laws were removed from the record, and every wrong thing in the life of the individual was nailed to the Cross as the Lord Jesus bore them in His own body.

There was quiet in the kitchen. There had been some noise of spoons and pans and lids being handled in the preparation of the meal, but all of this quieted down. We concluded that the wife was listening to the conversation, and so we kept our voices raised. I asked Mr. Manchester about 1 Peter 2:24, which reads, "Who his own self bare our sins in his own body on the tree, that we, being dead to sins, should live unto righteousness; by whose stripes ye were healed." Did Peter mean to tell us that Jesus bore all the sins from the cradle to the grave, or just part of the sins? Did Jesus have a mental reservation when He died for us, and did he decide in His own heart that He would not die for all the sins, but only for those up to a certain point in our lives, after which we would be on our own? My host said very vigorously, "That could not possibly be. Jesus did not work with mental reservations. All His words and ways and actions were transparent. He did not do a halfway job when He became our Saviour."

By this time the conversation had become so interesting to Mrs. Manchester that she came into the parlor carrying the dish towel in her hands, and she said to me, "What you have been telling my husband is most interesting to me. I wish I could have been with you here in the parlor and heard all the conversation." Then she sat down as though she intended to get the matter settled in her own soul and not be bothered with cooking, nor making coffee, nor preparing salad. The welfare of her soul was evidently more important than the welfare of her body.

I said to her, "How many sins do you think the Lord Jesus bore in His body, I mean your sins? Did He die for all of them? Did He bear all of them, and if not, where did the efficacy of His work cease? Where does the Bible tell you that the Saviour died for just some of your sins and not for all? Let me ask you also, Mrs. Manchester, did the Lord Jesus die for you because you were good or because you were bad? And let me ask you also, did He give His life for you on the basis of your behavior in the future? Did He tell you in His Word that His death and the shedding of His blood would be of value only so long as you behaved and kept the law to the best of your ability?"

You would have enjoyed looking at the face of this friend as I asked her these questions. She was astonished and surprised and a bit upset. Her husband very discreetly remained silent but was sending a prayer to heaven that the light of God would be shed abroad in the heart of his wife. He did not pray in vain, for, as I watched her when she sought to answer my question, I saw that the light of God had revealed to her the sufficiency of the risen Christ on the throne and that she was just then trusting Him because of His wonderful work at Calvary.

She rose from the chair, went over to her husband, and said, "George, I have been absolutely wrong, and you were right. I did not realize that only Christ could save; I thought it must be Christ and me. I thought that if I did my best for God, the Saviour would make up the difference. How wrong I have been." She turned to me with deep gratitude and a sigh of relief as she expressed the peace that had now come into her heart. She said to me that she had never in her life realized how plainly the Scripture revealed our helplessness and the Saviour's sufficiency.

We had a wonderful supper together, and all through the meal, and sometimes with tears, she told us of the way she had been deceived, and the wonderful peace she now enjoyed.

Mrs. Fox Did Not Like It

Mrs. Fox changed from being a bitter enemy to being a devoted friend, and the circumstances surrounding this change are so very interesting I am happy to tell you the story.

I was conducting a revival meeting in a country schoolhouse which would seat about seventy or eighty people. It was in a farming community, and practically all of those who came were farmers with their wives and children. The meeting was not under the supervision of any particular church, and since it was held in the schoolhouse and not in a church building, friends from different denominations felt free to come.

Among those who came quite regularly to the services was a Catholic family by the name of Murphy. Mr. Murphy was a very quiet man but very thoughtful and with an analytical mind which did not move very rapidly toward a conclusion. Besides Mr. Murphy there was his good wife, a short, red-haired woman with a happy smile; Bobbie, the twelve-year-old son; and Betsy, a fourteen-year-old daughter. They all came to the services. Mr. Murphy was so pleased with the presentation of the gospel that he persuaded his aged mother to come and also his sister, with whom the mother lived.

Night after night all of these friends came and came early in order to be sure to get a seat. They said very little, but they paid very close attention to the preaching, and I could see that they were very receptive in their attitude. The old mother was the first one to see that Christ Jesus was God's real and only Saviour for her. She trusted Him with her soul. Mr. Murphy was the next to accept Christ. I had come to his house at his request to have a meal with the family at the noon hour.

As we stood out in the yard looking over his farm, I said, "Earl, you have a wonderful wheat field here. You will get a great crop from it this year."

"No, Dr. Wilson, you are mistaken," he replied, "this field is about forty percent tares."

"I see no tares," I said, as I looked carefully over the forty-acre field. "I do see some cockle burrs or some bright green weeds over yonder to the right, but I see no other tares."

My friend saw at once that I was not much of a farmer, and he said, "You do not recognize tares when you see them. This field is mostly tares."

This statement rather surprised me, for I thought that tares were weeds, and so I said to him, "Where are there any other tares besides the patch of weeds which I see in the distant part of the field?"

He reached down by my side and picked up a handful of stalks which seemed to be nothing but wheat. As he handed them to me, he said, "These are all tares, Dr. Wilson. They were growing right beside you, and yet you did not recognize them because you did not know."

"How do you know these are tares, Earl?" I said. He was very happy to answer me, for he saw that I needed instruction concerning the characteristics of tares.

He explained as follows: "You see, Dr. Wilson, that this plant looks exactly like the wheat. The roots are the same, the stalks are the same, and so are the leaves and whiskered heads at the top. Now, if you will just open up the little pods on the head of the stalk you are holding, you will find that they are all empty." As he said this he began to open the pods with his thumbnail, and I was quite surprised to find that they were all empty just as he had said.

"Earl," I said, "I wonder if you are like this. Are you just a tare? You look like a Christian and you act quite like a Christian, but perhaps you are empty in the sight of God because you have not received the Lord Jesus Christ. Is that the case? 'He that hath the Son hath life.' "

His reply came very quickly. "Yes, you told the truth, Dr. Wilson, my heart is empty and so is my life, but right now I will take the Lord Jesus Christ. I have known for some time that I had only an empty profession, but this illustration has brought it home to me so strikingly that I must accept the Lord Jesus right now, and I do take Him."

Shortly after this his wife was saved, then both of the children, and a few days later the sister who lived with the aged mother. These, of course, began to write to their friends about their newfound life and to tell those whom they met what had happened to them. They had new life in their souls.

Mr. Murphy had a sister in southern Missouri to whom he wrote the story of his own salvation and also told about the others who had trusted Christ.

This sister was a devoted Catholic and was greatly incensed at the reports which she was receiving in the mail. She felt that some undue influence had been brought to bear upon those whom she loved dearly and that, whatever this influence was, it needed to be dealt with sternly and severely. She wrote a very strongly worded letter to her brother telling him that he and the others in the family must positively repudiate this entire business and stay by the Mother Church.

She said that unless they did recant and return she would come up herself and effect revenge on that preacher who had presumed and dared to change their faith. Mr. Murphy did not answer this letter, and so after three or four days the irate sister arrived on the scene. Mr. Murphy had told me about his sister, but he did not know then that she was coming, and neither did the rest of us know it.

One evening at the opening of the service, I saw a very fine-looking young woman sitting in the very back seat at the rear of the schoolroom, with a notebook and lead pencil. As I spoke of the finished work of Christ, mentioned who

He is and the virtues of His precious blood, this stranger
listened most attentively and even forgot to take notes because
she was so interested in the spoken word. My message was
John 1:12: "But as many as received Him, to them gave
He power to become the sons of God, even to them that
believe on His name."

I did not know that this stranger had come for the express purpose of injuring the preacher and of breaking up
the meeting, but it was so. She had told her brother that
she would put the preacher to flight and that she had come
up to this service for the very purpose of wrecking it.

As I sought to exalt the person of Christ Jesus and spoke
of His sufferings and His willingness to save, her heart was
deeply touched. At the close of the service I announced an
old hymn which we had used a great deal in that particular
series of meetings. The words read like this:

Again the blessed gospel I have heard,
That Word divine and true;
And God again has spoken to my soul:
Oh, what shall I do?

I had closed my eyes as I led the singing of this hymn
and was praying that the Holy Spirit would make the word
effective in every heart. Mrs. Fox had listened so attentively
that I prayed for her that she might see Christ Jesus as the
Saviour, escape the wrath of God, and become one of God's
dear children.

As I was directing the music with my eyes shut, suddenly
I became conscious that someone was standing near. I opened
my eyes to see who it might be and found this strange lady
standing, smiling and with her hand held out for a friendly
clasp.

I took her hand in mine and said, "Would you like
to accept the Lord Jesus tonight in the presence of all of
these friends?" She answered, "I have already accepted Him,
Dr. Wilson. I took Him for my Saviour while you were
preaching and while I was sitting back there in the seat. I
came forward just now in order to tell you about it and
to make my confession before all of these friends and relatives

of mine." Although this was a bashful little lady from the farm and had never made a public appearance before an audience on any previous occasion, her fears were banished this night, for she had trusted Christ, and this gave her holy boldness.

I thanked God for her coming, and in a few moments Mr. Murphy and his family had surrounded her to show their deep appreciation and to express to her their joy for her conversion.

The next day Mrs. Fox told me her story. She came up to this city and this service with the intention of forcibly making the preacher leave her relatives alone. She was prepared to do bodily harm, if necessary, to chase away the man who had so wickedly devastated the Catholic Church and other organizations by his preaching.

"Now, Dr. Wilson," she said, "although I did come up to harm you, and I did intend to break up the meeting because I thought it was contrary to God's will, I now see the wonderful blessing of God in giving His Son to die for me as described in the Bible last night. The Lord has won my heart. I can see the wonderful change in the lives of my brother and sister and the family of my brother. This thing is certainly of God, and I praise the Lord that He let me come up to the meeting, even though my intentions were very wicked indeed."

The entire family was now in happy fellowship with the Lord and with each other. God in a wonderful way saved each one, uniting them to His Son and to His own great Church.

Reader, it may be that you are an enemy of the gospel just because you do not know what the gospel is and perhaps because you have not seen the blessed fruits that follow the believing of that gospel.

I cannot tell how precious
The Saviour is to me;
I only can intreat you
To come, and taste, and see.

The Cursing Barber

The nicest, cleanest barber shop in town was located on the north side of the square opposite the county courthouse. Almost the entire front of the shop was plate glass, giving an unobstructed view of the entire interior of the shop.

Scotty, the barber, had equipped the shop with the finest of barber equipment, placed mirrors in various parts of the room, and had a table for reading matter, on which were the current issues of popular magazines.

Scotty was a very wicked man—anti-Christian, anti-church, antireligious—and was vigorous in his opposition. He was a militant enemy of the Christians in that little western city. When a Christian would walk past his shop and would be seen by Scotty, he would at once curse and swear, holding up religion to ridicule and calling down anathemas on the heads of the Christians. He was known all over the county as one who was an enemy of the church, an enemy of the preachers, and one who was definitely opposed to Christian ministry and teaching.

Scotty was not an old man—he was probably around forty-five years of age and had a lovely Christian wife and two splendid children, a boy and a girl. Scotty did not hinder the attendance of his family at church services, but he would have nothing to do with it himself, would have no Bible visible in the house, and would mock at the messages brought home by the family. Apart from his antagonism to the church,

Scotty was a pleasant, honest man. He paid his bills promptly, he did not gamble or drink, and he would boast that he was just as good as any of these hypocrite Christians that he knew in the town. On every other subject except Christianity, he would converse freely and rather intelligently.

With those who had no interest in Christianity, he would play chess or checkers in the shop while waiting for customers. He was such a good man as a barber, that even some of the Christians would go to him when they needed a barber. The merchants of the city had confidence in him because he met his obligations promptly and made a good name for himself in the business world.

The praying Christians in the town were constantly telling the Lord about this one who was God's enemy and their enemy. They knew that the Word of God had wonderful power to "break the rock in pieces" and would soften the hard heart. They were wise in their dealings with him and constant in their prayer for him. The Christian groceryman who served Scotty's family and the Christian dentist who took care of those needs in the family would speak kindly to Scotty about the Saviour. Sometimes through the mail Scotty would receive unusual gospel tracts containing warnings and invitations to Christ. He would glance at these and then destroy them, sometimes with an oath. The pastor of a neighboring church would sometimes go to the shop for service in order to seek some strategic opening for the gospel. The barber was very careful to avoid this issue, except to vent his feelings against the Christian religion, which he called a fraud and a farce.

One day in the early fall, Scotty's customers noticed a roughness in his voice. When he spoke, it was a bit harsh and not clear and pleasant as it had been. Scotty thought that he had a cold and purchased from the drug store some throat lozenges. He used these all day for several days, but the condition of his throat did not improve. As the hoarseness increased, his wife persuaded him to consult a physician. It seemed to the doctor that this was just a persistent cold which he could remedy by a stronger treatment. He did what he thought was best, but the throat continued to get worse. Scotty himself was disturbed about this and felt that he should have a more thorough examination than he had received. The physician also was impressed with the seriousness of the case and decided to have a secretion of the throat examined by a laboratory. He took a specimen from the throat, a specimen which he considered adequate, and sent it to the state hospital which was not too far distant. After a few days the answer came back—*cancer*.

Soon the word was spread around the town that Scotty the barber was afflicted with cancer of the throat. Of course, his business began at once to fall off. Men were afraid to have him breathing on them while cutting their hair or shaving. Parents were afraid to send their children to the shop for fear of being contaminated. Even his best friends gradually stopped coming for service because of the fear of being affected by his disease. (This response was, of course, foolish, since cancer is not contagious.)

The local physician was not equipped to treat the cancer with anything effective but sent him to a neighboring city where he could receive the usual treatment for such a disease. Scotty drove to the hospital two or three times a week for treatments, but none of these were sufficient to stop the ravages of the cancer. Gradually his voice failed as the vocal chords were involved, and he was unable to converse.

About this time, I passed through that little county seat and stopped to visit the county engineer, the superintendent of roads, on my way to conduct a service. While there I was invited to remain for supper, which I was glad to do. During the course of the meal my friends told me about the precarious condition of the barber and suggested that I go to see him. This I did. I found Scotty sitting in the kitchen, his mouth and throat covered with bandages and all the other evidences of the cancer plainly visible.

I introduced myself to him and said, "I am a physician from Kansas City who is deeply interested in the bodies and the souls of those who are sick. I came to tell you, Scotty, about a Man who loves you." Scotty shook his head to tell

me he did not believe it. I may say at this point that Scotty
could swallow neither water nor food. He was slowly dying
of starvation. I continued my conversation with him and said,
"I know you have not been friendly to Jesus Christ, nor
to His Bible, but that very Bible tells how the God of heaven
loves you, even though you have been His enemy, and He
wants to fix you up so that you can come to live with Him."
Again Scotty shook his head in denial. I said, "Scotty, I know
you do not believe it, but let me read to you the Saviour's
own words: 'For God so loved the world, that He gave his
only begotten Son, that whosoever believeth in him, should
not perish, but have everlasting life.' " I read it to him slowly,
quietly, but with definite purpose of heart so that he would
get every word.

Scotty listened intently, and then I continued, "Scotty,
God gave the Lord Jesus to you to save you. He did not
come to save good people but wicked people. Let me read
this to you: 'While we were yet sinners, Christ died for the
ungodly.' Scotty, the Lord Jesus wants you to believe His
Word, come to Him with all your sin, and trust Him with
your soul. The Lord Jesus said, 'Him that cometh unto me,
I will in no wise cast out.' " By this time, the tears started
down the face of our friend. He closed his eyes a few moments, then he pointed up toward heaven and then toward
his heart. Again he pointed to heaven and then placed his
hand on his heart. He shook his head in approval, for he
could not speak and was telling me in this way he accepted
Christ Jesus into his heart. I then said to him, "This man
receiveth sinners, and eateth with them." A sweet peace filled
the heart of Scotty. His wife broke into tears of joy as she
saw that this one, who had rebelled against God and refused
God's messengers, was now trusting the One whom he
formerly had hated.

The news quickly spread around that Scotty had become a Christian. The believers who had avoided him
now came with their Bibles and with words of comfort to
pray with this newborn babe. He did not live very long to
tell the story, but those who came saw his confession as he

pointed heavenward and then placed his hand upon his heart, while the tears of repentance streamed down his face. He had trusted the Prince of Peace, and peace filled his heart.

They Met in a Restaurant

Louise was a lovely blonde with a host of friends but with a retiring disposition. She was admired for her talents, her gifts, her beauty, and her attractive personality. She went to church on Sundays and enjoyed the fellowship but did not enter into the Christian activities. She was not too well acquainted with her Bible, but she read it occasionally and found it to be too dry and uninteresting to hold her attention. She held an important position in the office of a contractor and builder, and her ability soon brought about a promotion which caused the other members of the office force to be quite jealous of her. This feeling distressed her so much that she resigned and sought work elsewhere.

The place which she subsequently found was one in which she received a larger salary and was entrusted with much more important work to do. After some weeks she discovered to her sorrow that the influential members of that firm belonged to a faith which was not at all acceptable to Louise. These friends did not force their religion on her, but they made it quite evident that she should join them and participate in their religious exercises. This daily warfare gave Louise quite a heartache. She rejected completely that which their religion taught them and would respond by various Scriptures which she had learned as a child and from the various pastors to whom she had listened.

At noon Miss Louise usually ate her lunch at a very attractive restaurant near the place of her employment. Another young woman about her age also ate her lunch in this restaurant, and Louise was attracted to her because she seemed to be one of the same sort as herself. This young lady always bowed her head and expressed her gratitude to God before eating. Louise had not seen this done before, no other persons in the restaurant did it, and she really admired the courage of this one who publicly gave thanks to God.

Several days passed by without either of these speaking to the other. Finally, Louise said to the young lady, "Why do you bow your head at the table before eating?" The answer came rather reluctantly, for this person was very retiring in her nature and did not easily make friends: "I am a Christian and believe that we should be thankful to God first for the Saviour and then for the food He gives to us. Each time I go to the table, I thank the Lord for being so good to me and for providing the food for my needs." This testimony affected Louise quite deeply. She compared this new friend with herself. She had every blessing heart could wish and yet was not grateful to God. After this she and her new friend conversed at the table at each noon hour. The new friend did not tell Louise about the Saviour, did not explain the gospel, and made no effort to help Louise spiritually.

One day Miss Mabel, the new friend, asked Louise what she was going to do for the summer vacation. Louise replied that she had made no arrangements and did not know just what she would do. Mabel then suggested that they go together for their vacation and spend two weeks at the Lakes. This suggestion appealed to Louise, and she agreed that they would arrange to go together for this outing. The arrangements were completed, and they left together for an anticipated time of joy and fellowship at the lake resort.

They arrived at the resort on Sunday morning. I had been having a week of special services at this vacation spot, for it was a Christian camp where the Word of God was taught mornings and evenings, but many forms of entertainment were available. She heard different persons on the grounds talking about some special messages I had given during the previous week, and Louise expressed a desire to learn more about the subjects that were discussed. Friends told her that perhaps she could find some of my books in the gift shop located in the hotel. She went to this store and was told that all of my books had been sold except one, a copy of *The Romance of a Doctor's Visits,* and this one had the covers torn off. She could purchase it for five cents. She bought the book and went out on the lawn under a shade tree to read it. As she read it, the Holy Spirit revealed to her that "all her righteousnesses were as filthy rags." She noticed also that salvation is a gift, for "the gift of God is eternal life."

The effect of the messages that she read left her in tears. As she sat weeping with the book in her lap, a missionary passed by, a friend who was home on furlough, and, seeing her distress, went to her side. She told him that she would like to be saved but did not know how. He at once presented to her the Lord Jesus about whom she had been reading and explained to her that, since God sent the Lord Jesus to save her, she should permit Him to do it. He quoted to her, "Come unto Me all ye that labor and are heavy laden, and I will give you rest" (Matt. 11:28). He called her attention to Luke 19:10: "The Son of man is come to seek and to save that which was lost." He also told her that "Christ also hath once suffered for sins, the just for the unjust, that He might bring us to God, being put to death in the flesh, but quickened by the Spirit" (1 Pet. 3:18).

Louise was ready for the message, she realized her need, she saw from the Scriptures that the Lord Jesus came to save her, and so she trusted Him with her soul and believed in Him as her Lord and Saviour. Smiles replaced the tears, peace replaced the turmoil, and she rested in Christ Jesus, the living, risen Saviour. The rest of her days at this Bible conference were spent in earnest and devoted study of the Scriptures as she learned more and more of the loveliness of Christ and the precious truths of the Scriptures. She returned to her work with a new joy and with a new message for her friends. This lovely Saviour is still available to any who read this story and have not yet found the peace the heart hungers for.

A Birth Between the Rails

A great evangelistic meeting was in progress in C————, Illinois. The evangelist in charge sent me a hurried call to come at once to see him. My train arrived at C———— in the early morning at five o'clock, in a dense fog, making it impossible for me to see any object whatever as I alighted from the train.

Leaving me standing beside the track, in absolute darkness and with no knowledge whatever of the location of the depot nor of the town, the train pulled out of the little village. As I walked along the track, feeling my way cautiously, I finally found the platform and the station, for the density of the fog with which I was enveloped necessitated my walking very slowly. The windows and the doors of the depot were closed, and the weather was cold. I therefore sat down, huddled up in my ulster, and awaited the break of day.

About seven o'clock, the sun appeared through the clouds and revealed the form of a man walking along the road near the station, carrying a dinner bucket. Hailing the gentleman, I welcomed his cordial response, as he inquired whether or not he might render any assistance to me as a visiting stranger.

"Is the Rev. H———— now preaching in this city, and can you tell me where he is stopping?" I asked.

"I am sorry," he replied, "but the meeting has been moved up to A————, and the evangelist is there this week. It is only three miles up the track, and I am working

up there in the roundhouse. If you will walk along with
me, I will show you the house in which the preacher is being
entertained."

Gladly I accepted the invitation and started to walk up
the railroad track with the new friend. The conversation that
followed was frequently interrupted, both of us stopping now
and then to discuss some point or seeking to remove some
doubt.

"What kind of a preacher is the Rev. H————?"
I asked.

"He is a wonderful man" was the response. "He has
the whole country stirred up in these parts, and many have
been converted."

"Did you get converted in the meetings?"

"No," said the friend, "God will not save me. Several
times I went to the mourner's bench, and I have talked with
the preacher, and I have prayed, but God will not have me."

Seeing that this splendid man, standing six feet four
inches—a physical giant—was in deep soul trouble, I immediately took him by the arm and said, "Would you like
to be saved right now?"

"Do you mean right on this railroad track? Nobody
gets saved on a railroad track; you have to be in a church."

"You did not answer my question," I remarked. "Tell
me, do you want to be saved right now?"

"Indeed I do," he answered, "more than anything in
the world; I do wish God would save me right now."

Again the question was asked, "Would you like for the
Lord Jesus to save you right now?"

Quickly the answer came, "Do you mean all by Himself? He cannot do it without my help."

"But," said I, "have you not tried to help Him for several
weeks and failed? Why do you not let the Saviour do it
for you? Let me show you." Whereupon I produced my
Bible, turned to Isaiah 53:5, and with my tall friend looking
over my shoulder, slowly read the passage: "But he was
wounded for our transgressions, he was bruised for our
iniquities."

"Wait a minute, mister," he said. "Who is that verse about?" To which I replied, "It is about Jesus Christ and you."

A look of astonishment came over the face of this new friend, as he said, "Do you mean that Christ was taking the punishment for *me*? Did He really die for *me*? Was it *my* sins He was being punished for?"

"Yes, my friend," and turning quickly to 1 Peter 2:24, we read slowly and carefully, "Who his own self bare *our* sins in his own body on the tree."

A look of happiness and peace appeared in the face of this hardworking mechanic, and, quickly looking heavenward, he said, "Lord Jesus, I never knew before that it was *my* sins You were dying for, and it was *me* You came to save. Thank You Lord Jesus; I believe it, and I believe You; and You are *my* Saviour."

Picking up the dinner bucket and the satchel which had been sitting on the railroad ties, we resumed our journey, while I continued giving to the mechanic further revelations of the value of the Lord Jesus Christ. I quoted, "He that hath the Son hath life" (1 John 5:12) and explained that because Christ Jesus had been received, therefore eternal life had been imparted. Many other truths also were presented, and when we came to the village of A————, we parted to meet again the same evening at the church where special meetings were being conducted.

Finding the evangelist at the hotel, I took care of his needs, supplied what was necessary, and then was invited to attend the evening service since my train did not leave until quite late. This I was glad to do that I might see what testimony would result from the morning experience with my friend.

At the close of the evening service, when the evangelist called for testimonies, the workman from the roundhouse quickly arose and, facing the congregation, said, "Friends, you all know what a bad actor I have been in this neighborhood. You know how I have tried to get religion but never could find peace. Now I am happy to say to you that this day has been a heaven on earth to me. This morning as I left my home at C————— in the fog, I met this doctor who is our guest tonight. Taking his Bible, he showed me that Jesus died for me, bore my sins away, blotted them out, and gave me eternal life. I trusted Him between the rails—right out on the railroad track, and I praise God tonight I am born again and have peace in my soul."

With joy in my soul, I left the service that night to board the train for my homeward journey. The joy came because the Holy Spirit had revealed Christ to this seeking sinner. There was also a sadness in my heart because the evangelist had failed to make the way of salvation clear and plain. Let me urge every teacher and Christian worker to present Christ Jesus clearly in His Person and Work in order that souls may not be left in the dark.

A Hopeless Cripple Could Sing

Achsah was a crippled girl who lived in a modest cottage on a very busy street. Her whole body was paralyzed so that she could only move two fingers on each hand and have a limited movement of the two arms. In seeking for some form of work to occupy her mind, she had learned to string beads and thereby make necklaces and bracelets. A kind friend had made a tray to set across her breast in such a position that she could pick up these beads of various colors and arrange them on strings in beautiful patterns. These bracelets and necklaces she sold to those who visited her and in this way was able to make a few dollars to help with her expenses.

The family of this afflicted girl was not very sympathetic with her. They gave her little attention and really criticized many things in her life, which gave her a very sad attitude and a very heavy heart.

One day a friend told me about this young lady and her affliction. My interest was aroused, and shortly thereafter I called to see her. I found a very attractive young lady, about eighteen years of age, and quickly saw that she had an unhappy home life and eagerly sought outside company for fellowship. We had a very nice visit together, as I admired her work and spoke of the very clever way in which she handled the beads, though she was so badly handicapped. She told me with some pride how she delighted to mingle the colors in the strands in order to obtain the best effect. She mentioned a number of friends who had purchased the beads from her and expressed their pleasure and gratitude at finding such beautiful articles to use for presents. Our conversation about these lovely articles led me to comment on Malachi 3:17, and I read the passage to her: "And they shall be mine, saith the Lord of hosts, in that day when I make up my jewels; and I will spare them, as a man spareth his own son that serveth him." This verse greatly interested Achsah, and she asked the meaning of it. Instead of answering her directly, I asked whether she was a member of some church, and she replied that she was and told me the name of the church. She added, "I am a member in that church of the Esther class, but they never come to see me, and neither does the preacher. A few people in the church have been to see me, but they never talk to me about the Bible or about God. They only tell me about the social events in which I have no interest. I am so glad you have come to talk to me about God and the Bible, for I often think of the meeting with God and wonder if He will be glad because of my handiwork, or whether something more is required."

This gracious invitation to tell her about our lovely Lord opened the door for my message. I began at the Scripture that we had just read and explained that the Lord makes us His children by purchasing us with His precious blood. Then He makes us His property by workmanship, so that He deals with us in our lives to make us the kind of people He wants us to be. We become "mine" by purchase, and we become "mine" by workmanship. Achsah was quite intrigued by this explanation and said, "I would like to belong to Him; will you tell me how?" To this I answered, "Let me read to you John 1:12: 'But as many as received him [the Lord Jesus], to them gave he power to become the sons of God.'" I then explained to her that when any person takes the Lord Jesus to be the Lord of his life and the Saviour of his soul, he at once comes into God's family and becomes one of God's jewels. I sought to make it clear to her mind and heart that jewels are made by God. Only He can make a ruby, a sapphire, or a diamond. All she would need to do would be just to accept God's gift, the Lord Jesus, and at once that blessed Lord would make her one of His jewels. In order to help her further, I remarked that God polishes jewels after He makes them, but He does not try to polish pebbles and stones. They are not worth it.

This whole story was so new to Achsah that she was unable to grasp the truth clearly, but she promised me to think it through and hoped that I would come back to explain it to her more fully. A few days later I returned to see this interesting girl. I found her waiting for me and expecting me. As I sat down beside her, she said, "Tell me that story again, Doctor, the one you read in the Old Testament." I read the passage to her from Malachi 3:17 and said, "God, the Father, will give you to the Lord Jesus for Him to give you a place in His family, make you one of His jewels, then give you the robe of righteousness, and give you the gift of eternal life so that you will be His child." I then quoted to her 1 John 5:12: "He that hath the Son hath life." At this point Achsah showed in her face that a new light had dawned in her heart. She said rather excitedly, "I see that wonderful truth. God gave Jesus to me, so that He could make me one of His jewels. I love that, and I am so happy to take Jesus for myself. I want Him to make me a shining, lovely light for His glory." Her joy was beautiful to see. The perplexing problem of her life had been solved, and she was rejoicing in this new relationship with the precious Saviour.

Achsah lived about a year after this wonderful event. Those who came to see her remarked on her lovely faith, and the happiness that seemed to fill her heart. At each opportunity she told them that she had met the Saviour, and He had made her His jewel. When she found that the day of her departure was at hand, she requested her family to have me conduct the service at the church, which I was glad to do. The group known as the "Esthers" were present at the funeral, and each one was dressed in white. As they passed the casket, each one dropped a flower upon her breast. When

I told the story of her conversion to the group, I could see a strange look of surprise and doubt on some of their faces. They had thought that because she was so patient in her suffering, and so thoughtful and kind in her attitude toward others, that therefore she was always a Christian. They could hardly believe it that this beautiful girl needed salvation. There are still those who think that building a good character is equivalent to being a Christian. The Word of God, however, clearly states, "Except a man be born again, he cannot see the kingdom of God."

Lost on Mount Wilson

Every situation in life has the attention and care of the Holy Spirit. Christians in general believe that the Holy Spirit is active in the matter of dealing with souls for their salvation and in dealing with Bible students for their illumination. It is not so generally known, however, that the Spirit is active also in directing the steps of the children of God and in overruling circumstances for their blessing.

On one occasion, accompanied by my friend, George, we visited the observatory on the top of Mt. Wilson. We were desirous of learning some of the mysteries of astronomy, and, if possible, of having the privilege of gazing through some of the large telescopes at the wonders of the heavens. We derived much enjoyment from our journey and felt that we had received a great deal of benefit from the visit to the observatory. The night was spent on the crest of a mountain, from which lofty eminence we expected to observe the rising of the sun in the early morning hours. This we did. Beneath us lay a sea of billowy clouds which obscured the valley below. The sun appeared over the great mountain peaks to the east like a huge red ball of fire. It was a marvelous sight and well worth the long climb up the steep slopes.

Having eaten our breakfast, prepared and packed for us by our hostess the night before, we decided that it would be most interesting to investigate the back side of this great mountain and see what we could find on the way down to the bottom of the ravine, some five or six miles away. We soon discovered a trail which was plainly marked by a rough signboard, bearing the name "Rattle Snake Trail." It seemed quite a well traversed track when we first left the summit of the mountain, but it soon led to a very steep and tortuous passage through the brush, and we had difficulty finding the trail as we slowly descended. After traveling for about an hour, picking our way slowly through treacherous and difficult places, we found to our dismay that we had lost the trail completely.

George had brought with him for use on our journey a water bottle filled with water, and out of our breakfast we had saved a little food. The day was unusually hot, and the sun beat down upon our heads mercilessly. The mountainside was so very steep that our feet were continually sliding down into the toes of our shoes, causing blisters which became quite raw and very sore. We wandered here and there, seeking vainly to find the path again. Our efforts proved futile, for it could not be found. There were no marks of any kind to direct us on our journey, nor were any houses to be seen, nor any sign of human life.

As we wandered here and there seeking a way out of our predicament, we finally found ourselves on a ledge about fifty feet wide and covered with a thick growth of very tough bushes, through which it was very difficult to make our way. Suddenly, we discovered that immediately in front of us was a deep chasm, with a sheer drop to a gulch about two hundred feet below. We retraced our steps and found that at the rear of this ledge was a steep cliff ascending several hundred feet above us. How we arrived in such a difficult situation we could not comprehend. Certain it was that we were there and in a predicament from which we knew of no way of escape.

In our perplexity, George and I knelt together in a small clearing and told our Lord that we were lost. We pleaded our helplessness and His supremacy. We were wholly cast upon Him for deliverance, and so we committed our cause to the One whom we had learned to know and love. We knew that the Holy Spirit was ever present to guide the feet of the children of God, to direct their ways, and to keep them for Himself. We were happy thus to trust this difficult matter to the One who had delivered us so many times in our Christian experiences.

Scarcely had we ceased praying, when we heard a rustling among the bushes. Whatever was causing this commotion we could not figure out. Nearer and nearer came the sound, and we were somewhat disturbed in our minds as to just what it was that was hunting us out. As we stood gazing in the direction from which the sound came, suddenly there sprang into view through the brush the form of a man dressed in khaki and bearing badges on his breast and on his hat, indicating that he was a government guide. With what joy we greeted him, and how gladly we told him our names and described our predicament! "How did you know we were here?" I inquired. "We were just praying that the Holy Spirit would bring someone to our rescue. We had scarcely ceased praying before we heard the sound of your approach, and we certainly rejoice that you are here. The Lord surely heard our prayer at once and answered quickly. Do tell us how it is that you found us."

There was an amused expression on the guide's face as he answered our inquiry. "My lookout hut is located across the canyon on a projecting promontory. From this vantage point I can observe with my field glasses most of the paths in these woods. When you men started down Rattle Snake Trail from the top of Mt. Wilson, I immediately started after you, for I knew you would never make it to the bottom. No one ever descends the entire length of that path successfully. At the top of the mountain, the trail is quite distinct, but it gradually becomes more indistinct, and very few travelers who are enticed by it ever succeed in keeping on it. That is the reason I started at once to find you. I knew just about where you would be lost."

Our hearts were filled with gratitude as we expressed to the guide and to God our thanksgiving. We remembered the Scripture, "Before they call, I will answer" (Isaiah 65:24).

This our Lord had done for us. He knew we would be lost and therefore had already arranged the guide for our salvation. We told the guide of the thoughts that were going through our hearts. We sought to tell him of the Guide sent from heaven for our eternal salvation. But our message did not meet with a very happy reception, for he was not interested in spiritual matters.

"Will you show us the way out?" we asked.

"No," said the guide, "I will not because I cannot. There are no marks to direct you, and there are no signs at all, so that I cannot give you any instructions. But if you will follow me, I will *take* you out. I know these woods perfectly but cannot tell another. You come along with me, and I will soon put you on the trail again."

Quickly our minds recalled John 14:6—"I am the way, the truth, and the life: no man cometh unto the Father, but by me." Christ did not come to *show* us the way. Christ *is* the way. He will *take* us through life and bring us to God, but He will not be a "Wayshow-er," for we are unable to follow either instructions or directions. Again, we told the guide of the wonderful similarity between the salvation he was bringing us from the woods and the salvation the Saviour brought us from our sins.

We followed our guide closely, never losing sight of him once along the way, and enjoyed stories of his experiences in finding other travelers who were lost and helpless in the woods. So we follow Jesus Christ and receive from Him the precious stories in His Word of His wonderful dealings with others, as He led them out of the darkness of unbelief into the narrow path that leads to life.

Soon we were at the path again and pursued our downward journey. Our throats were parched with thirst, our feet were very sore with blisters, but our hearts were rejoicing because we had been found. The guide left us to return to his lookout. How blessed it is that our heavenly Lord does not leave us! He cannot leave us safely to ourselves, for we would soon lose the way and be off the path again. He has said, "I will *never* leave thee, nor forsake thee" (Heb. 13:5).

As we neared the bottom of the steep descent, we heard the noise of water as it rushed over the stones on its way down the valley. The noise was tantalizing. We started to run, and after about two blocks we found a stream of delightful, cold water, fresh from the snows of the mountaintop. Falling down on the bank, we drank until we were fully refreshed. Again, we remembered the precious Word of God, which said, "As cold waters to a thirsty soul, so is good news from a far country" (Prov. 25:25). We had both of these, for the good news was the coming of the guide and the cold waters we found in this delightful stream.

There in those attractive surroundings of mountains, trees, and loneliness, we knelt to pour out our hearts to God in thanksgiving and praise. The Holy Spirit had watched over us with loving care. We were safe from harm and refreshed in spirit. The remainder of the homeward journey was enriched by songs of praise, and, when we arrived at our destination, we were happy to recount the gracious care of our God and His love for His two children.

Hints and Helps for Personal Soulwinners

I. For Use with the Unsaved.

    A. For the Atheist and Infidel.
              Mark 16:16. He that believeth not.
              Ps. 14:1. The fool hath said.
              2 Cor. 4:3. If our gospel be hid.
              John 8:43, 44. Ye are of your father.
              John 12:48. He that rejecteth me.
              Acts 13:40. Beware, lest that come upon you.
              John 3:19. Men loved darkness.
              Luke 11:35. Examine your light.

    B. For Those "Too Bad" to Be Saved.
              Acts 13:38, 39. Be it known unto you.
              Col. 2:13. Having forgiven you all.
              1 Pet. 3:18. Christ hath once suffered.
              Heb. 7:25. Able also to save . . . uttermost.
              1 Tim. 1:15. He came . . . to save sinners.
              Rom. 4:5. He justifies the ungodly.
              John 3:16. Whosoever believes . . . has life.

    C. For Those Who Are Trying to Save Themselves.
              Job 40:12-14. God's confession.
              Titus 3:5. Not by good works.

Isa. 64:6. Our righteousness as rags.
Eph. 2:8, 9. By grace, not by works.
Rom. 3:28. Justified by faith.
Rom. 4:5. Justifies the ungodly.
Rom. 4:6. Righteousness without works.

D. For Those Who Don't Realize They Are Lost.
Rom. 3:19. All the world is guilty.
1 John 5:19. The world lies in wickedness.
Rom. 3:23. All have sinned.
Eccles. 7:20. Not a just man upon earth.
1 Tim. 5:6. Dead while she liveth.
Ps. 51:5. Born in sin.
Rom. 5:12. All have sinned.
John 3:3. All need the new birth.

E. For Those Who Fear They Cannot Hold Out.
John 10:28, 29. They shall never perish.
John 17:12. Christ will keep His own.
1 Pet. 1:5. Kept by the power of God.
2 Tim. 1:12. He is able to keep.
Heb. 7:25. Christ ever intercedes.
Deut. 33:27. Underneath are God's arms.

F. For Those Who Need a Personal Application.
1 Pet. 2:24. He bare our sins.
Gal. 2:20. He loved me.
John 9:38. Lord, I believe.
Isa. 53:5. Wounded for our transgressions.
John 1:12. As many as received Him.
John 3:16. A personal gift—Life.
Isa. 44:22. Blotted out thy sins.
Exod. 12:5. Your lamb shall be.
Matt. 16:15. Whom say ye that I am.

G. For Those Who Endeavor to Keep the Law.
Gal. 3:10. Cursed for not keeping all.
James 2:10. He is guilty of all.

Rom. 3:28. Saved without deeds of the law.
Rom. 3:20. Not justified by deeds.
Rom. 5:20. The law entered; the offense abounded.
Rom. 7:4. Dead to the law.

H. For Those Who Desire Forgiveness
Eph. 1:7. In Him we have forgiveness.
Luke 7:48. Thy sins are forgiven.
Mark 2:10. Christ has the power now.
Acts 10:43. Receive remission of sins.
Acts 5:31. Christ gives forgiveness.
Dan. 9:9. To God belongs forgiveness.
Ps. 130:4. There is forgiveness with God.
1 John 2:12. Your sins are forgiven.
Eph. 4:32. Forgiven for Christ's sake.
Exod. 34:7. God forgives iniquity.

I. For Those Who Are Not Certain of Judgment.
Acts 17:31. God has the day appointed.
Jude 6. The judgment of the great day.
Eccles. 11:9. Bring thee into judgment.
Eccles. 12:14. Every work is to be judged.
John 5:22. The Son is appointed Judge.
Acts 24:25. Felix trembled, and—
1 Tim. 5:24. Going before to judgment.
1 Pet. 4:17. Judgment must begin.
2 Pet. 2:3. Judgment lingers not.
2 Tim. 4:1. God will judge all.

II. For Use with Believers

A. For Those with Heavy Burdens.
1 Pet. 5:7. Cast your care upon Him.
Ps. 37:5. Commit thy way unto Him.
Ps. 81:6. God will remove your burden.
Isa. 53:4. He hath borne our griefs.
Matt. 11:28. Christ will give you rest.

B. For Those Who Need Assurance.
  Heb. 13:5. He will never leave you.
  John 3:16. You will never perish.
  John 6:37. He will not cast you out.
  John 10:9. You shall be saved.
  John 10:28. They shall never perish.
  1 John 3:14. We know we have life.
  1 John 5:13. We may know we have life.
  Isa. 43:25. He blots out our sins.
  John 17:12. Christ is the keeper.
  2 Tim. 1:12. We know He is able.
  2 Tim. 2:13. He abideth faithful.

C. For Those Who Have Drifted and Wandered.
  Luke 15:11-32. The prodigal son.
  John 6:68. To whom shall we go.
  Matt. 11:28. Come unto me, heavy laden.
  John 7:37. The thirsty are invited.
  John 6:35. The hungry are invited.
  Philem. 17. Receive him back again.
  Ps. 23:3. He restoreth my soul.

D. For Those Who Are in Sorrow and Grief.
  Isa. 43:2. If you pass through the waters.
  Ps. 25:2. Let me not be ashamed.
  Isa. 53:4. He hath borne our griefs.
  Ps. 63:5. My soul shall be satisfied.
  Ps. 84:12. The blessing of trusting.
  Isa. 48:18. Thy peace like a river.
  Ps. 81:16. Fed with the finest of wheat.
  1 Pet. 5:7. He careth for you.

E. For Those Who Desire Consecration
  Rom. 6:13. Yield yourselves unto God.
  Rom. 8:14. Led by the Spirit of God.
  Rom. 12:1. Make a present of your body.
  John 4:14. The upspringing well.

John 7:38. The outflowing river.
John 15:16. The fruitful vine.
Gal. 2:20. Christ liveth in me.
Phil. 1:21. To live is Christ.
Eph. 5:18. The Spirit-filled life.